Celebrations

Celebrations

The Cult of Anniversaries in Europe and the United States Today

William M. Johnston

Transaction Publishers
New Brunswick (U.S.A.) and London (U.K.)

First paperback printing 2011
Copyright © 1991 by Transaction Publishers, New Brunswick, New Jersey.

This book is printed on acid-free paper that meets the American National Standard for Permanence of Paper for Printed Library Materials.

Library of Congress Catalog Number: 90-11240
ISBN: 978-0-88738-375-5 (cloth); 978-1-4128-4233-4 (paper)
Printed in the United States of America

Library of Congress Cataloging-in-Publication Data

Johnston, William M., 1936–
    Celebrations: the cult of anniversaries in Europe and the United States
    today / William M. Johnston.
        p. cm.
    Includes bibliographical references and index.
    ISBN 0-88738-375-0
        1. Anniversaries. 2. United States—Popular culture—History—20th
    century. 3. Europe—Popular culture—History—20th century. 4. Post-
    modernism—United States. 5. Postmodernism—Europe. I. Title.
E169.12.J645   1991
394.2—dc20   90-11240
                                                                    CIP

TO MY BELOVED WIFE,

CLAIRE

*Ancestor worship's a form of self-seeking: all the same, one
Is grateful to those who had no immediate hand in our crazy
Present.*

— C. Day Lewis, *An Italian Visit* (1953)

Contents

Preface
Anniversaries as Apprenticeship for the Bimillennium

This book started as a study of the theory and practice of anniversary commemorations in Europe and the United States during the 1980s. As a historian attending conferences in Western Europe and the United States, throughout the decade I noticed how many symposia, exhibitions, television shows, and newspaper articles invoked anniversaries for their justification. From the 500th anniversary of the painter Raphael in 1983 to the bicentennial of the American Constitution in 1987 to the bicentennial of Mozart's death in 1991, an astonishing number of cultural events today take their origin in an anniversary. Some unfold worldwide like the tricentennial of Bach, Handel, and Scarlatti in 1985 or the bicentennial of the French Revolution in 1989, and some occur locally like the tricentennial of Philadelphia in 1982 or the bimillennium of the German city of Bonn in 1989.

The more I examined the range and depth of cultural commemorations during the 1980s, the more I became convinced that they deserve a general explanation. When and where did the cult of anniversaries originate? Why has it flowered during the 1980s? Why does it take different forms in Western Europe than in the United States? How much longer will it last? These are some of the questions that this book addresses.

As I proceeded to compare European and American commemorations, I became aware that the heyday of anniversaries during the 1980s has coincided with the rise of the mentality known as "postmodern." In exploring how anniversary commemorations fit postmodern assumptions, I hit upon a major theme of the book: the cult of anniversaries reinforces the concerns of postmodernism. Whether postmodernism is defined as a mode of creativity that refuses to vie with previous avant-gardes, or simply as a playful recombining of disparate elements, it finds anniversaries an ideal vehicle for reassessing past authorities. We commemorate what we no longer wish to emulate.

Having connected the cult of anniversaries with the rise of post-modern consciousness, I began to weigh a more daunting question: Does the cult of anniversaries shed light on what will follow postmodernism? Nearly every writer on contemporary culture agrees that postmodernism is a transitional phenomenon. To label a mentality in relation to its predecessor is to suggest planned obsolescence. Even the most ardent postmoderns do not expect that mentality to prevail for long. Yet a characteristic of postmodernism is reluctance to speculate about what lies ahead. Openness to every nuance of opinion deters postmoderns from specifying future directions. By relying on the calendar to set priorities, the cult of anniversaries exemplifies post-modern distrust of authority, and such a lack of direction reinforces the refusal to predict a next stage.

Postmodernism probably cannot last much longer, at least not without a new name, yet few of its devotees wish to speculate on what will ensue. A study of the cult of anniversaries can fill this gap in two ways. First, because anniversaries depend on the calendar, they dramatize time's on-ward march. The cult of anniversaries makes one so keenly aware of shifts in taste that it forces one to ask how much longer post-modernism can endure. Second, the calendar holds a surprise in store for everyone. The 1990s will culminate in an unprecedented event: the end of the second millennium and the arrival of the third. As soon as one starts to imagine how the shift from 1999 to the years 2000 and 2001 will affect attitudes worldwide, one can see that the Great Climax will evoke, however fleetingly, some kind of new consciousness. The years 2000 and 2001 will unleash preoccupation with crisis and renewal sufficient to put postmodernism in the shade. It seems not unlikely, therefore, that postmodernism will one day be seen as a transition to bimillennial consciousness.

The cult of anniversaries interlocks with the bimillennium not least because that calendric shift will incorporate multiple anniversaries within it. During the year 2000, people will commemorate the arrival of the first millennium in the year 1000, as well as the turn of the years 500 and 1500, not to mention the inception of the notion of *anno domini* in the mid-sixth century. By contemplating this prospect I arrived at the major thesis of the book: the surest way to forecast the impact of the bimillennium is to examine the cultural anniversaries that will precede it. The bimillennium will evoke an unprecedented response, not least because cultural anniversaries have proliferated so widely during the years preceding it. The years 2000 and 2001 will be experienced as the climax of a quarter century of historical celebrations. The assumptions that characterize anniversary commemorations during the 1980s and 1990s will culminate in unheard of extravaganzas during the year 2000. That is why the cult of anniversaries is worth examining now, before the onset of the bimillennium starts to reshape it.

Having begun as a study of the contemporary cult of anniversaries, this book evolved to include proposals on how to make forthcoming anniversaries enrich the bimillennium. Part One analyzes reasons for the popularity of anniversaries during the 1980s, connecting them with postmodernism, with the need for long-term rhythms, and with the quest for national identity. Contrasts in modes of cultural planning between Western Europe and the United States loom large in this analysis, as does the role of commercial interests in shaping a "commemoration industry." Part Two applies categories from Part One to the task of planning anniversaries during the 1990s. It proposes ways to use anniversaries more imaginatively so as to prepare for the bimillennium and to exploit the ferment that the end of a calendric era will bring. If Part One connects the cult of anniversaries with postmodernism, Part Two connects it with bimillennial consciousness.

The book addresses everyone who is concerned about the fate of culture today. Planners of commemorations will find much to ponder here, as will cultural commentators of every stripe. Sociologists, historians, and scholars of religion will find their categories applied in a novel way. This is the first book to interpret cultural anniversaries as characteristic of our time. It examines many instances from the 1980s and proposes almost as many for the 1990s. Above all, it argues that cultural anniversaries meet deeply seated needs for regularity within the flow of time and that these needs will intensify as the bimillennium approaches. To understand the cult of anniversaries may be the best tool we have for easing the transition from postmodern permissiveness to bimillennial intensity.

This book aims to anticipate requirements of the 1990s by interpreting practices of the 1980s. If some of the proposals seem ahead of their time, such boldness only emphasizes the challenges that the Bimillennium will bring. Cultural anniversaries mark pauses in the march of time,

1

Anniversaries during 1988:
Opportunities Seized and Missed

What is an Anniversary? Why Are Anniversaries Important?

The late 1980s have abounded in assessments of the state of culture, both in Europe and the United States. Observers from every ideology and academic field agree that the present age suffers disarray and cries out for reorientation. Not often before have so many educated people devoted so many words to charting where a culture stands and where it may be headed without achieving thereby a clear sense of direction. Never before have the riches of the past been displayed in such diverse venues to so many different publics as in Europe and the United States today. Never before have so many people enjoyed such ready access to the accomplishments of every region and past.[1]

The label "postmodern" has emerged as a term to describe the present state of culture, in which former avant-gardes have lost their authority and former styles blend together to offer an unprecedented range of options both old and new. Blending of previously incompatible styles, doctrines, and methods characterizes postmodernism, in fields as diverse as art, literature, scholarship, advertising, and politics.[2] Postmoderns delight in combining what their predecessors kept apart. As ideologies fragment, doctrines undergo montage, so that ideas from previously hostile sources now cohabit in delight. Some critics like Jean-François Lyotard deplore the disruption of knowledge that results from jettisoning authority, while others like Stephen Toulmin want to reorient knowledge toward more individual ends.[3] By re-

3

fusing any longer to emulate modernity's avant-gardes, postmoderns enjoy a chance to heal the wounds that ideology inflicted.

Notwithstanding unprecedented efforts to interpret our age, observers have overlooked one of its salient features: people today package the past in bundles labeled "anniversary." Any famous person who enjoys a 50th, 100th, or other anniversary in multiples of fifty of his birth or death is almost certain to have a commemoration mounted during that year. The same holds true for any event, particularly the founding of a city, mode of government, or corporate enterprise. In Europe the observance of cultural anniversaries has become both a cult and an industry. During the 1980s between fifty and a hundred major cultural anniversaries, both of individuals and events, have been celebrated each year in the five most anniversary-minded countries, namely Britain, France, Germany, Austria, and Italy. The annual total exceeds one hundred if one includes anniversaries celebrated by smaller towns, and this figure does not count commemorations held in countries like the Netherlands, Belgium, Spain, or Greece. Sheer abundance makes the phenomenon of cultural anniversaries one of the major features of our time.

An anniversary commemoration of a major figure customarily involves several elements. Almost invariably, sponsors invite academic specialists to present papers on the celebrand and his era at one or more conferences. In 1983 Franz Kafka, for example, received no less than eight centenary conferences held on three continents. Often boosters in a celebrand's home town organize a display of visual materials such as paintings, prints, photographs, and books. Such a montage may travel around Europe as well as to American universities. In the case of a painter or architect there may be several museum exhibitions involving loans from around the world. In 1983, during the same year as the Kafka conferences, the painter Raphael received at least a dozen 500th anniversary exhibitions in Europe and North America. Many of them published catalogues as well. In addition, a significant figure or event is likely to inspire one or more documentary films, and in Europe almost any celebrand is guaranteed discussion on television and radio, as well as in the daily press. Every day nearly every major European newspaper devotes one or two pages to "culture," and on these pages anniversaries inspire as much as half the coverage. In a word, anniversaries dictate timing across the whole gamut of cultural production.

The commercial opportunities generated by anniversaries have brought into being a commemoration industry. Publishers schedule the marketing of books, both scholarly and popular, to coincide with anniversaries. The bicentennial of the French Revolution, in a paroxysm of opportunism, unleashed hundreds of titles, ranging from reprints of multivolume series to trendy popularizations. In addition, major historical events generate the production of souvenir objects, including T-shirts and every sort of memorabilia. Nineteen eighty-nine will be remembered in France not least as the year when *Le Journal des guillotinés,* listing 17,500 victims of the guillotine, could be purchased at any street corner. The bicentennial had the further effect of causing French music to predominate at European festivals throughout 1989. In sum, anniversaries serve the purposes of commerce, scholarship, and government about equally.

Journalists in particular have adopted anniversaries as a convenience for packaging a wide variety of topics. Figures who receive no official commemoration can count on receiving newspaper stories on their birthdays. Columnists in the United States play what may be called "the numbers game" by invoking anniversaries, including odd ones like a 32d or 180th, as a gimmick to connect stories to a given day. Sports writers resort to this device with bewildering frequency. Anniversary-fever runs riot with events generated by mass culture, such as the fiftieth anniversary during November 1988 of the broadcast of Orson Welles's version of *The War of the Worlds.* This media event was recalled across the United States with exhibitions, conferences, memorabilia, and reenactments. Many anniversaries, particularly ones concerning television, sports, and celebrities, serve no other purpose than to justify media coverage.[4] This book largely ignores campaigns by the media to commemorate its own earlier creations.

During the 1980s the quantity and lavishness of cultural commemorations increased more rapidly in Europe than in the United States. Civil servants in Western Europe use anniversaries to schedule cultural events to a much greater extent than do academics in the United States. Although no country celebrates all the anniversaries that crop up in a given year, Europeans exploit far more of them than do Americans. Because Britain, France, Germany, Austria, and Italy lead the world in commemorating cultural anniversaries, any study of the phenomenon needs to concentrate on these countries.

Since no one has studied Europe's cult of anniversaries, commentators have overlooked the clues it provides to the mentality of our age, and specifically to postmodernism. Postmodern sensibility expresses itself not least through the cult of anniversaries. Although recourse to anniversaries originated in the late eighteenth century, their proliferation since the 1970s coincides with the emergence of what, for lack of a better name, is known as postmodernism. Postmoderns commemorate what they no longer wish to imitate.

Useful as it is to connect the cult of anniversaries with postmodern trends, it is even more enthralling to speculate how the next decade will affect the conduct of anniversaries. The major cultural event of the late 1990s will be the coming of the bimillennium in the years 2000 and 2001. Mass media as well as universities worldwide will publicize the ending of one millennium and the coming of the next. This anniversary will differ from others because the turn in the calendar touches all inhabitants of the globe. However fleetingly, the bimillennium will trigger convergence between obsessions of mass culture and those of intellectuals. If one regards the bimillennium as an unusually comprehensive commemoration, one begins to grasp how anniversaries during the 1990s can help people prepare for that climactic one. The abundance of anniversaries since the 1970s will predispose Europeans and Americans to experience the bimillennium as the ultimate commemoration.

This book examines, then, the phenomenon of cultural anniversaries as they have evolved in Britain, France, Germany, Austria, and Italy since the 1970s. Cultural celebrations in these "superpowers of anniversaries" will be compared with historical commemorations put forward in the United States. Contrasts between Europe and the United States constitute a major topic of the book, with a view to explaining why Europe honors luminaries while the United States prefers events. Countries like the Netherlands, Belgium, Spain, and Greece will be mentioned only in passing, while the increasing attention paid since 1986 to anniversaries in the Soviet Union will not be covered. The use of Soviet and East European anniversaries to exploit *glasnost* deserves separate treatment.[5]

Certain conventions govern cultural anniversaries in ways that need to be clarified at the outset. By universal consent, major anniversaries occur in multiples of fifty years from the year of the birth or death of a celebrand. In others words, it is 50th, 100th, 150th, 200th, 250th, and larger fifty-year anniversaries that get commemorated. Except for events from the immediate past, anniversaries of a 10th, 25th, 75th, 125th, or 175th recurrence arouse little interest and play a minimal role in this book. By common agreement, cultural luminaries include writers, artists, composers, scholars, scientists, or other creators whom organizers deem important enough to honor after they have died. Commemorable political events embrace a wide range, including wars, treaties, accession or death of monarchs, gain or loss of national territory, and the enacting of major legislation. Anniversaries of the founding of cities and of governmental regimes attract the most support. It should be noted that decisions about who or what deserves commemoration lie not with the public but with cultural managers. Because it is managers who shape anniversary commemorations, this book deals in large measure with the policies and status of these entrepreneurs.

The emergence of global interdependence in economic life has increased the popularity of anniversaries. The interlocking of economies through telecommunications, transnational corporations, and worldwide advertising makes it essential for each country to proclaim its national identity ever more clearly to its citizens. At a time when images, news, and fashions get distributed worldwide, each nation needs to remind its taxpayers of their distinctiveness. Precisely because the interlocking of the world economy threatens to submerge national identity, governments must work harder to foster it. The usefulness of anniversaries in promoting national identity constitutes a major theme of the book.

To cite one much publicized example, now that France is becoming ever more intertwined with its old rival Germany as well as with the rest of Europe, the government needs to remind Frenchmen of what makes them different from Germans and everyone else. No better way to do so could be imagined than to spend 1989 commemorating the French Revolution as the legitimating myth of Republican France. The French government spent several hundred million dollars to commemorate the Revolution at national, provincial, and city levels, as well as in more than fifty foreign countries. Thousands of civil servants and businessmen labored in hundreds of venues in order not merely to provide entertainment and instruction, but to remind Frenchmen and the rest of the world what it is that sets France apart. The bicentennial of the French Revolution affirmed French national identity. In so doing it counteracted the impact of images and products flooding in from the global economy. In a world whose growing interdependence makes it more urgent than ever for each nation to articulate its identity, anniversaries provide one of the most efficient and exhilarating means of doing so.

To show how anniversary commemorations have proliferated, this chapter will inventory the principal ones that took place during a representative year, namely 1988. This "review of the troops" concerns the six countries that the book addresses, namely Britain, France, Germany, Austria, Italy, and the United States. Because hardly anyone has surveyed even one year's quota of commemorations, almost no one realizes the scope of the phenomenon. Ignorance prevails partly because sponsors have nothing to gain by publicizing one another's initiatives. Anniversary commemorations tend to unfold in isolation as though each enjoyed a monopoly throughout its year. To counteract this, Part Two of the book urges cultural managers to devote more energy to coordinating commemorations. As a foretaste of such possibilities, the outline of opportunities seized and missed during 1988 will suggest some of the benefits that greater cooperation among sponsors could have fostered.

Great Britain

Anniversary commemorations in Britain during 1988 were dominated by two political events: the Spanish Armada of 1588 and the Glorious Revolution of 1688–1689. The Conservative government of Margaret Thatcher seized both occasions as a means to proclaim national identity. The Armada was recognized through an exhibition at the Naval Museum in Greenwich, and through a recreation of London in 1588 at Tilbury Fort on the lower Thames, as well as through the usual spate of books and souvenirs. There was also an exhibition in Belfast, Northern Ireland, where remains of many sunken Spanish ships reside.

The Glorious Revolution, which in 1688 deposed James II and in 1689 brought the Dutch leader William III and the Stuart Queen Mary II to the British throne, plays somewhat the same role for England's constitutional monarchy as the French Revolution does for France's republic. Both events supply legitimating myths for the current regime, myths that historians have increasingly discredited. Since through the so-called Declaration of Right (1689) the Glorious Revolution guaranteed civil rights to male citizens in the North American colonies as well, it is one of the few European anniversaries that Americans claim as their own. This complex heritage was celebrated through joint Anglo-American conferences held in early 1989 in Williamsburg, Virginia, and Washington, D.C. The Dutch commemorated their contribution by mounting a show on the "Anglo-Dutch Garden in the Age of William and Mary." Although the tercentenary of William and Mary culminated with a visit by Queen Beatrix of the Netherlands to London in July 1989, none of these happenings excited the British public.[6]

As luck would have it, the year 1988 also brought anniversaries of two distinguished English men of letters who rank as critics of the Glorious Revolution. The philosopher Thomas Hobbes (1588–1679), who dedicated his life to the defense of absolute monarchy, would have detested the so-called Glorious Revolution, while the poet Alexander Pope (1688–1744) lampooned the Whig governments that emerged from it. Although Hobbes and Pope were commemorated through individual conferences held both in Britain and the United States, no one thought to proclaim the irony of having their joint anniversary coincide with that of the Glorious Revolution. To interweave Hobbes, Pope, and the Glorious Revolution would have placed all three in a vivid new light. The omission may be explained by the fact that the bulk of commemorations for the Glorious Revolution took place in 1989 rather than 1988. Nor did anyone exploit the anniversary of the death of John Bunyan (1628–1688), the author of *Pilgrim's Progress* (1678, 1684), in order to discuss how the era of religious strife memorialized by Bunyan ended with the Glorious Revolution. Bunyan died in the very year that the kind of persecution he had suffered ceased in England (albeit not, alas, in Ireland). This is the sort of conjunction between anniversaries that cries out to be exploited.

During 1988 the British reacted to a number of other religious anniversaries with varying degrees of enthusiasm. The founder of Methodism, John Wesley (1703–1791), saw the 250th anniversary of his conversion in May 1738 celebrated with great fanfare, while his brother, the hymn-writer Charles Wesley (1707–1788), got overlooked. Likewise, the 500th anniversary of the birth of Miles Coverdale (1488–1568), who as an early translator composed some of the most memorable phrases in the English Bible (particularly in the psalms), seems to have gone unheralded. Potentially more awe-inspiring was the 1000th anniversary of the death of Saint Dunstan (c. 909–988), who restored monasteries in England. Although the Dunstan Millennium was commemorated with a conference at Canterbury, its relative neglect elsewhere illustrates the obstacles that attend commemorations of Christian luminaries. Likewise the Catholic writer Ronald Knox (1888–1957) received only the scantest attention during his centenary year. Chapter 9 will propose ways of honoring such figures better.

In the visual arts, the 200th anniversary of the death of one of England's greatest painters, Thomas Gainsborough (1727–1788), occasioned no major exhibition. It was recognized instead at a number of smaller museums including the Dulwich Picture Gallery and the Gainsborough House in Sudbury. By way of contrast, the watercolorist and nonsense-author Edward Lear (1812–1888) received a couple of exhibitions, including a lavish one at Brighton. Surprisingly, the National Gallery seems to have ignored the 150th anniversary of the opening of its building on Trafalgar Square in 1838, whereas the City Art Gallery of Leeds celebrated its centennial with a show of 101 objects, one from each year of its existence.

Almost every year Britain has a bevy of major writers to commemorate. The year 1988 brought acclaim above all to Lord Byron (1788–1824), to the American-born poet and critic T.S. Eliot (1888–1965), and to T.E. Lawrence (1888–1935). All of them received one or more conferences and a torrent of publications, while Lawrence was honored with a show at the National Portrait Gallery and another at the Bodleian Library, Oxford. Byron was honored by several small shows in Paris as well. Alexander Pope (1688–1744), however, received much less attention, apart from a show at Orleans House, London, about his Twickenham residence, while Matthew Arnold (1822–1888) got almost no recognition.

Moreover, scholars of English history like the Liberal G.O. Trevelyan (1838–1928), the legal historian Sir Henry Maine (1822–1888), the biographer John Morley (1838–1923), and even the historian of eighteenth-century political elites Sir Lewis Namier (1888–1960) fared rather badly. The British expend far less energy than do the French or the Germans honoring scholars. Even the great astronomer Sir William Herschel (1738–1822), who discovered the planet Uranus and otherwise transformed the science of astronomy, got short shrift. In

Germany or Austria he would have been hailed as a national hero; in Britain during 1988 he was just another forgotten name from the eighteenth century.

By way of contrast, the popular press in Britain celebrated the centennial of the most notorious murders in the annals of London. Because "Jack the Ripper" ranks as a hero of popular culture, the 100th anniversary of his five slayings in London's East End received much fanfare between July and November. Two other heroes of folklore were feted by book publishers, if not by academic conference-givers. James Stuart, the Old Pretender (1688–1766), saw the 300th anniversary of his birth fall in the same year as the 200th anniversary of the death of his son, the Young Pretender, Bonnie Prince Charlie (1720–1788). No fewer than five biographies of Bonnie Prince Charlie appeared during 1988. Public figures who got overlooked during 1988 included the Marquis of Cornwallis (1738–1805), who governed India and Ireland before negotiating peace with Napoleon at Amiens in 1802, and Sir Robert Peel the Younger (1788–1850), who gave his nickname to the London bobbies in 1828 before leading repeal of the tariffs on wheat known as the Corn Laws in 1846. *Sic transit gloria mundi.* As all these examples show, no amount of achievement suffices to prompt a commemoration unless an anniversary figure finds managers to back him. Today that is most likely to happen to figures who evoke national identity.

Considering how many anniversaries Britain overlooked, it is worth mentioning that the Republic of Ireland mounted, or perhaps one should say concocted, a major anniversary during 1988. The city of Dublin observed its 1000th anniversary. For those who wondered what exactly was being commemorated in a city founded around 800, it turned out to be the capture of the city from the Norse by a Celtic leader named Mael Sechnail in 988. A generation later the Norse occupiers were ousted for good at the battle of Clontarf. In a word, Dublin celebrated the 1000th anniversary not of the founding of the city but of its recapture by Celts. Nothing could better illustrate how cultural managers use anniversaries to promote national identity amid a global interdependence that undercuts it. Just as Mrs. Thatcher's government urged citizens to identify with victory over the Spanish and with the cementing of parliamentary rule, so Ireland invited its citizens to revel in the prowess of the Celts.

A major commemoration both inside and outside the British orbit was the bicentennial of the founding of English settlement in Australia. That nation's year-long celebration deployed the entire resources of the culture industry, both at home and abroad, ranging from books and television programs through conferences and exhibitions to tourist attractions and memorabilia.[7] Like many lesser events, the World's Fair in Brisbane concentrated on luring tourists. Commercial benefits did not, however, impede the clarifying of Australian national identity through the joint efforts of media, universities, museums, and even the theater. Australian visual arts received worldwide acclaim, particularly through shows of Aboriginal painting held in New York, London, and throughout Australia. Last but not least, through a succession of exhibitions in London, Oxford, and elsewhere the Australian bicentennial obliged a previously reluctant Britain to acknowledge its former colony's achievements. New Zealand, by way of contrast, did not attempt a comparable extravaganza when two years later it celebrated the 150th anniversary of the Treaty of Waitangi, which transferred sovereignty from the Maoris to Britain. New Zealand had to respect the sensibilities of the Maoris, who even so in February 1990 threatened the Queen's visit with violence. By stimulating discussion of national identity through thousands of events, the Australian bicentennial provided a model of how to commemorate a nation. Ingenuity in hitching every kind of cultural endeavor to the bicentennial showed that in today's world nothing succeeds like a well-planned anniversary.

France

In France during 1988 all other anniversaries were overshadowed by preparations for the bicentennial of the French Revolution to be held the following year. The cities of Rennes and Grenoble mounted major shows on France in 1788. Such preparations did not, however, prevent cultural figures from receiving the usual attention during their anniversary. No other country rivals France in its zeal to proclaim that every generation since at least the eleventh century has produced a galaxy of talent. Each year's crop of anniversaries embodies a chain of achievement in art, literature, music, religion, and learning that runs for at least a thousand years.

In literature, 1988 marked the 300th anniversary of the dramatist Pierre de Marivaux (1688–1763), whose comedies have been a staple of the Comédie Francaise since the 1790s. Needless to say that venerable theater commemorated one of its own with performances throughout 1988. The master stylist and natural historian, the Comte de Buffon (1707–1788), who coined the saying "Le style est l'homme même" (1753), received a major exhibition at the Paris Museum of Natural History, while the philosopher Nicolas Malebranche (1638–1715), who developed Descartes' philosophy into a full-blown metaphysics, was noticed by only a few professionals. Among recent writers, the Catholic novelist Georges Bernanos (1888–1948) proved too reactionary to command national attention. He was commemorated only by fellow partisans.

Musical performances worldwide during 1988 recognized the 150th anniversary of the composer Georges Bizet (1838–1875), whose orchestral works were performed with greater frequency in 1988 than in perhaps any previous year. Hardly anyone, however, dwelt on the pathos of Bizet's early death, which came just before his opera *Carmen* broke through to acclaim. One of the most popular of all composers died thinking himself a failure. No commemoration can compensate for that. In 1888 the hymn of the Communist movement, the "Internationale," was first performed in the city of Lille. The text came from the pen of a French writer, Eugène Pottier, during the Paris Commune of 1871 and was republished in his *Chants révolutionnaires* (1887), while the music came from the hand of a worker in Lille by the name of Adolf De Geyter. Although in 1988 the Communist movement stood at its lowest ebb since the nineteenth century, the debut of the "Internationale" was duly reenacted, perhaps to honor Lille rather than Marxism.

It was an unusually thin year for commemorations of visual artists in France, since the celebrands worked in genres that most people ignore. The portrait-sculptor David d'Angers (1788–1856) was overlooked except in his native city of Angers, which boasts a museum dedicated to his works. The portrait-pastellist Maurice-Quentin La Tour (1704–1788) received scant national attention, while the Lorraine-born engraver Jacques Bellange (1594–1638) was recognized through part of a show in Meaux. Not even France could mobilize its cultural infrastructure to awaken interest in masters of lesser genres.

As might be expected, commemorations that feted a town's place in history abounded. The city of Arles commemorated the centennial of Van Gogh's residence there in 1888, while the city of Nancy mounted a show to commemorate the founding of the "New City" by Duke Charles III in 1588. The Chateau of Saint-Germain-en-Laye commemorated an event that few would otherwise wish to remember, the inauguration of Louis XIV's residence there 350 years before.

Among political figures, one of France's most adept diplomats, the Abbé de Talleyrand (1754–1838), seems to have been largely overlooked during the 150th anniversary of his death. He suffered the handicap whereby exploits performed under a succession of regimes as different as the Revolution, Napoleon's Empire, the Restoration, and the July Monarchy do not suit France's legitimating myth. Talleyrand's talent for changing front is not one that French governments wish to commend, although he did receive an exhibition in one of the town halls of Paris during 1989. Perhaps Belgium should have commemorated the old fox for the role he played in negotiating the independence of that country from the Netherlands in 1830. For similar reasons the Fifth Republic, which General de Gaulle established in 1958, hesitates to commemorate politicians from the discredited Third Republic. That is why one of the latter's most distinguished figures, Léon Gambetta (1838–1882), went largely unheralded during 1988. Instead, the Fifth Republic exalted the centennial of an economics minister Jean Monnet (1888–1979), who ranks as an initiator of the European Economic Community. On his 100th birthday, the day after the presidential election in the United States and the same day as the anniversary of *Kristallnacht* in Germany, the ashes of Jean Monnet were exhumed from a cemetery near his retirement home and solemnly transferred to the Pantheon in Paris. This was France's way of taking credit for the emergence of the European Community.

During a year when Dublin was celebrating its 1000th anniversary of liberation from the Vikings, the city of Strasbourg was celebrating the 2000th anniversary of its founding as a Roman camp in 13 B.C. In keeping with their obsession with continuity, the French mounted pageants, conferences, concerts, and half a dozen exhibitions to celebrate Strasbourg's role at the crossroads of French and German conflict and reconciliation. Yet no amount of panache could conceal an irony underlying the festivities. As the seat of the European Parliament, Strasbourg was celebrating its venerability at a time when its legislators were implementing a political and economic integration that threatens many of Europe's traditions. Amid euphoria over reconciliation between Germany and France, perhaps someone should have recalled that in 455 Strasbourg was destroyed by Attila the Hun. Its subsequent rebuilding recalls a quality that abounds in Europe, namely the capacity to begin again. As the unification of the European Community accelerates toward a deadline of December 1992, Europeans once again are beginning anew. That is one reason why anniversaries are more necessary than ever.

Germany, Italy, and Austria.

[handwritten: Different depending emphasis on country.]

German anniversaries exalt culture above politics. The year 1988 brought a bevy of cultural anniversaries that hardly anyone outside of Germany noticed. The 500th anniversary of the pre-Reformation humanist Ulrich von Hutten (1488–1523) was marked with a conference and an exhibition. Three major figures born in 1788 received conferences: the philosopher Arthur Schopenhauer (1788–1860), the poet Joseph von Eichendorff (1788–1857), and the poet Friedrich Rueckert (1788–1866). The latter is best known for settings of his poems by Franz Schubert as well as by Gustav Mahler in the *Kindertotenlieder*. The painter Albrecht Altdorfer (c. 1480–1538) received an exhibition in his hometown of Regensburg as well as in Berlin, while the modernist Oskar Schlemmer (1888–1943) received a centenary exhibition in Basel, Switzerland. In a gesture typical of European municipal pride, the town of Augsburg honored its rococo ceiling-painter Matthäus Günther (1705–1788). The composer C.P.E. Bach (1714–1788) received a modicum of programming worldwide during his death-bicentennial, while Max Bruch (1838–1920) had his works performed more than ever before. It comes as no surprise that the mystical philosopher Johann Georg Hamann (1730–1788) seems to have been ignored.

Among German political anniversaries, the small city of Meersburg on the northern shore of Lake Constance celebrated its millennium through a campaign of building restorations and a series of concerts, conferences, and publications. Across Lake Constance, the city of Konstanz commemorated the 150th anniversary of the inventor of the dirigible, Graf von Zeppelin (1838–1917). Prussian history generated several anniversaries during 1988. The Great Elector Frederick William (1640–1688) was celebrated with a conference, while the Emperor of a Hundred Days, Frederick III, who ruled the German Empire between March 9 and June 15, 1888, while dying of throat moreover, celebrated 900 years of the monastery of Saint John on the Island of Patmos. In contrast to the Russian millennium, this was noticed only by coreligionists, for as a rule, the world press does not fancy religious anniversaries.

The United States

A principal theme of this book is that the United States commemorates events rather than luminaries. Whereas each of the eight states that had ratified the Constitution in 1788 commemorated that event, few of 1988's opportunities to commemorate luminaries took hold. During a rich year for literary anniversaries, only one received major attention, that of the playwright Eugene O'Neill (1888–1953), whose works were performed nationwide. In America no less than in Europe, theater managers find anniversaries indispensable for programming. The contrast between Europe and the United States crystallizes around a writer like Henry Adams (1838–1918), who is just the sort of figure that Europeans exploit to articulate national identity. In France or Germany his anniversary would have evoked several major conferences, as well as radio and television debates, for *The Education of Henry Adams* (1907) is an ideal book to stimulate discussion of national identity. In the United States, however, Adams remains an elusive figure, known chiefly to specialists in American Studies, who accorded him a couple of perfunctory conferences. A cultural critic who in Europe would be a national luminary ranks in the United States as a regional curiosity. The failure of American scholars and entrepreneurs to seize an anniversary like that of Adams reveals how Americans ignore the proliferation of cultural anniversaries taking place in Europe. Americans simply do not celebrate writers, artists, and composers the way Europeans do. Much of Part One of this book is devoted to examining reasons for this difference.

Among other literary anniversaries in 1988, the double one of the deaths of the philosopher Bronson Alcott (1799–1888) and his daughter Louisa May Alcott (1832–1888) passed unnoticed. The 100th anniversary of the publication of Edward Bellamy's utopian novel *Looking Backward* (1888) was celebrated as an act of local boosterism by his hometown of Chicopee, Massachusetts, while the poet John Crowe Ransom (1888–1974) was recognized chiefly in the South. The French thinker Etienne Cabet (1788–1856), who founded a utopian community called Icaria in Texas and another in Illinois, was remembered only locally. Even the 150th anniversary of Ralph Waldo Emerson's "Divinity School Address" (1838) did not arouse excitement at Harvard Divinity School.

In the visual arts the 250th anniversary of the painter Benjamin West (1738–1820) was completely ignored, while the 150th of the New England architect Henry H. Richardson (1838–1886) got only the scantest attention. The Bauhaus painter Josef Albers (1888–1976), who taught for decades at Yale, did not receive a major exhibition in the United States, but he did in Tourcoing, near Lille. Apart from a couple of books, the Bauhaus architect Mies van der Rohe (1888–1969), whose glass towers transformed America's cities, received surprisingly little attention, either in the United States or in Germany.

In the realm of politics, two weighty anniversaries went almost unheeded: that of the first Governor of Massachusetts, John Winthrop (1588–1649), and that of President Eisenhower's Secretary of State, John Foster Dulles (1888–1959).

As might be expected, the world of popular culture celebrated its own. The detective story writer, Raymond Chandler (1888–1959), who created the figure of Sam Spade made famous by Humphrey Bogart, was feted in the press, as was the 100th anniversary of the poem "Casey at the Bat," which first appeared in the San Francisco *Examiner* in June 1888. By way of contrast, the 200th anniversary of Sarah Hale (1788–1879), who wrote "Mary Had a Little Lamb," was all but ignored.

As these omissions show, the United States lacks an infrastructure to mount nationwide commemorations of cultural figures. American writers and artists tend to get commemorated in their hometowns or homestates but not elsewhere. Local universities and societies mount conferences, which find little echo anywhere else. Local heroes serve to lure tourists but not to embellish the national self-image. For better or for worse, national identity in the United States hinges not upon publicizing creative geniuses, but upon celebrating founding events.

Notes

1. David Lowenthal, *The Past Is a Foreign Country* (Cambridge: Cambridge University Press, 1985), examines the "heritage industry" worldwide.

or priests, cultural workers became employees of the state and as such were expected to instil in citizens a sense of national identity. In France the state paid salaries to priests until the separation in 1905, and in Germany, Austria, and Italy the state still subsidizes churches in various ways.

The Napoleonic model of state-paid officers of culture who perform a "civilizing mission" underpins the ministries of culture that flourish throughout Western Europe. Cultural ministries in France and elsewhere gained prestige after 1959 when President de Gaulle appointed the visionary André Malraux to be Minister of Culture. For ten years Malraux strove to disseminate appreciation of Europe's, and particularly France's, heritage across all regions and social strata.[2] His use of the Ministry of Culture to enhance national and regional identity has been imitated all over Europe. In addition to activities as diverse as scrubbing grime off buildings (a practice that Malraux initiated), renovating museums, commissioning art, and promoting folklore, ministries of culture have embraced the cult of anniversaries as a means of furthering their goals.

In the United States, by way of contrast, private foundations play somewhat the same role as cultural ministries do in Europe. Funding for conferences, exhibitions, and films derives mainly from foundations in the United States, whereas in Europe these activities get funded through ministries of culture or their subsidiaries. In Europe the cult of anniversaries has emerged in the last thirty years as a means of establishing consensus among cultural ministries, intellectuals, and the public about each year's agenda of cultural events. In the United States private foundations feel no call to promote national consensus because it is not tax revenue but rather capitalist accumulations that fund them. Whatever anniversaries American foundations support, few of them do so because they wish to enhance national identity. Rather, foundations reflect the agendas of their founders and respond to proposals in this light. In the United States hardly anyone supposes that foundations should back causes that taxpayers can espouse. In the United States the government-sponsored National Endowment for the Humanities, like its rival for the arts, operates more like a foundation than like a European ministry. One of the chief differences, then, between the United States and Europe is that Americans rely on private largesse to fund the kind of initiatives that European states channel through cultural budgets. This state of affairs results from the separation of church and state (or in secularized terms of culture and state) that has marked the United States since its Constitution was written in 1787.

American academics, who labor under no obligation to address national agendas, often distrust Europe's system of patronage that hitches culture to the state. In fact, Europe's cultural ministries allow more leeway to intellectuals than outsiders might imagine. Almost the only prerequisite for intellectuals who receive stipends from the state is to address issues of national identity. In return for honoraria for appearing on state television and radio or at cultural programs of embassies, European intellectuals undertake to interpret, and even to personify, national identity. They may do so in any way that they choose, except to disclaim all national affiliation. One reason why the cult of anniversaries flourishes in Europe more than in the United States is that it seals the bond between intellectuals and the state.

In Europe anniversaries have become one of the chief means by which officials mobilize intellectuals to address matters of national and regional concern. The cultural figures being celebrated each year (whom we shall call celebrands) become carriers of national and regional heritage during that year. European intellectuals have become adept at debating contemporary issues through reference to such canonical figures. During the bicentennial of the French Revolution, for example, intellectuals found ways to relate nearly every issue of the 1990s to those of the 1790s, if only by emphasizing the discrepancies. Indeed, some commentators carved out a role denouncing the bicentennial. The game of invoking canonical figures finds few players in the United States because few Americans identify with intellectuals, either past or present. Whereas in America past creators command minimal allegiance, in Europe all educated people acknowledge that certain figures encapsulate national tradition in such a way as to illuminate the present. Anniversaries provide a device by which this roster of canonical figures gets repackaged each year.

Each European nation boasts a cast of historical characters, who get trotted out during anniversary years to dance a turn under the lights. The process whereby stars are chosen involves not the minister of culture or a battery of committees but rather what may be called the Great Calendar. The fact of when a creator was born or died determines when he or she will get revived. There is very good reason for resorting to something so arbitrary. Because Europe has no continent-wide ministry of culture to coordinate the national ones, the task of supervising cultural schedules exceeds the reach of any bureaucracy. In an arena where bickering is constant, a way to reduce conflict is to let the accidents of birth and death decide who will be honored. In the absence of a pan-European coordinating committee, the Great Schedule-Maker-in-the-Sky assigns a cast of luminaries for each year.

One of the few ways in which Europeans still acknowledge the play of chance in life is to rely upon the Great Calendar to set priorities of public discourse. The very arbitrariness of anniversaries reinforces their appeal. In general, postindustrial societies have striven to minimize the role of the fortuitous in everyday matters. Whatever can be subjected to rational control is so controlled.[3] The quality of manufacturing is monitored by computers and guaranteed by robots. News from everywhere is received instantaneously. Fruits and vegetables from every region of the globe are marketed throughout Europe as though geographical barriers no longer existed. Airline and train schedules are devised so as to mesh with one another, and occasional lapses only underline the efficiency of the system. Constraints caused by distance are diminishing to a vanishing point.

During an era when control over distance is growing, it comes as a surprise to learn that the cult of anniversaries emphasizes our lack of control over time. In the performing arts, whose execution involves regulating time in its flow, schedule makers rely unabashedly on anniversaries. In the world of classical music, for example, it is universally accepted among programmers, funders, performers, and audiences that the anniversary of the birth or death of a composer will be celebrated worldwide during that year. It is unthinkable that the anniversary of composers like Bizet in 1988, Moussorgsky in 1989, Tchaikovsky and Franck in 1990, Mozart and Vivaldi in 1991, or Rossini and Massenet in 1992 should go unobserved. So dependent are programmers on anniversaries that relatively neglected composers like C.P.E. Bach and Bruch in 1988, Paganini in 1990, and Meyerbeer in 1991 receive disproportionate attention in those years. Concert series, radio broadcasters, and summer festivals alike seize the opportunity to perform the entire output of celebrands. Radio announcers delight in commemorating performers of the past. Since music is the most international of arts, musicians can ignore national boundaries. During the bicentennial of the French Revolution, for example, festivals all over Europe featured the music of France.[4]

Musicians' reliance on anniversaries to regulate repertoire raises questions about parallel strategies in the visual arts. Although curators exploit anniversaries as routinely as musicians do, a fundamental difference divides the two realms. What links the two is a quest for consensus about priorities among planners, performers, and audiences. Anniversaries serve as a godsend to planners, publicists, and reviewers to justify each season's offerings. The cycle of anniversaries introduces an impersonal criterion to which all parties cheerfully submit. Anniversaries lubricate the wheels of planning.

What distinguishes scheduling in the visual arts from that in music is a scarcity of original objects to display. Even an artist as prolific as Picasso did not produce enough works for every major museum in Europe and the United States to have mounted an exhibition during his anniversary year of 1981. Whereas a composer's anniversary can be commemorated in every concert hall on the same day or throughout a single year, a painter's or sculptor's anniversary has to preempt a few venues that will pool resources. For musicians, anniversaries function as a device to market an elastic commodity, whereas for museum curators they help to allocate scarce resources. Anniversaries of composers inspire a proliferation of performances, while those of visual artists require concentration in a few sites.

Photographic images offer an escape from such constraints. The 150th anniversary of Daguerre's invention of photography in 1989 was one anniversary for which every museum could assemble originals. In the United States alone at least fifty museums mounted exhibitions of photographs during 1989. Moreover, during all artists' anniversaries photography facilitates the dissemination of images through catalogues and reproductions, so that any artist's anniversary results in photographs of his works being distributed through magazines, posters, and catalogs. Artists' anniversaries unleash a blizzard of photographic images in just the way that composers' anniversaries unloose a tide of performances. Chapter 4 explores in detail how the commemoration industry uses anniversaries to promote marketing.

The cult of anniversaries introduces an element of the foreseeable into cultural programming. Even planners of nonanniversary events gain from knowing what anniversaries will fall during a given year. Because so many cultural offerings in Europe coincide with anniversaries that can be anticipated years in advance, planners of other events know what they will be competing against. However arbitrarily, anniversaries inject an element of predictability into medium-range and long-range planning. Entrepreneurs who do not wish to conform to anniversaries can produce counterpoints to them. By submitting to the cult of anniversaries, programmers acquire a degree of control over the future.

Such expediency suggests a further reason why the cycle of anniversaries delights planners. A year's crop of anniversaries throws up arresting conjunctions among celebrands. When celebrands in a given year cry out to be compared, planners need no further justification for holding a joint commemoration. Anniversaries can be a godsend for collaborative projects. The year 1990 in the German-speaking world may be used to illustrate some of these possibilities. During that year a variety of painters who flourished between 1800 and 1848 shared anniversaries. In particular, it was the year of Biedermeier landscape painters, no fewer than four of whom enjoyed anniversaries either in 1989 or 1990. The principal painter in 1990 was Caspar David Friedrich (1774–1840), whose mystical depictions of German landscapes can be contrasted with the Italian ones of Karl Blechen (1798–1840). Although the planners could not have known it, such an exhibition would have coincided with the reunification of East and West Germany. In retrospect, their dual anniversary should have emphasized the fact that Friedrich flourished in Dresden and Blechen in Berlin.

Such a pan-German endeavor could have been enlarged to include two painters whose anniversaries fell the year before. Carl Gustav Carus (1789–1869) was a disciple of Friedrich, while Joseph Anton Koch (1768–1839) brought to perfection what is known as the heroic landscape. A four-man exhibition of these masters would have been a blockbuster offering an overview of German landscape painting between 1800 and 1840. The opportunity seemed even more piquant because the four painters could have been interpreted in light of a major literary anniversary, that of the Swiss novelist Gottfried Keller (1819–1890), who began his career as a landscape painter. Keller's major novel, *Green Henry* (1854–1855; 2d ed. 1879–1880) describes his evolution from being a landscape painter to becoming a writer. It contains some of the most lyrical passages on landscape in European literature. The conjunction of anniversaries in 1990 between Friedrich, Blechen, and Keller offered opportunities for interdisciplinary collaboration, only a few of which got exploited. Whether seized upon or not, the potential of such juxtapositions for generating new insights lends incisiveness to the cult of anniversaries.

European Affinity for the Arbitrariness of Anniversaries

These examples of how anniversaries help program concerts, coordinate exhibitions, and justify interdisciplinary endeavors illustrate benefits that accrue to producers and consumers alike. The examples rest on the assumption that in each country the cycle of anniversaries will each year throw up one or two major figures in literature, art, and music, as well as some in politics, thought, and science. The cult of anniversaries flourishes only because European countries have nurtured so many creators that each year supply outruns demand. To be sure, some years offer more than others, and perhaps not soon again will one year deliver a cornucopia in one field to match the quadruple anniversaries for Bach, Handel, Heinrich Schütz, and Domenico Scarlatti in 1985. Nonetheless, every year discloses more than enough cultural anniversaries for England, France, Germany, Austria, and Italy to enjoy an oversupply. Indeed, those countries vindicate their claim to be cultural great powers partly through their profusion of anniversaries. One thing that Europe will never run short of is figures and events to commemorate.

For everyone concerned, a basic appeal of the cult of anniversaries is its impersonality. Just as no bureaucrat dictates the years of a creator's birth or death, so no planner contrives the match-ups with other anniversaries that the calendar generates. By eluding human control, the cycle of anniversaries reminds us anew each year that however exceptional a creator's gifts may have been, he too had to be born and die. One can extend the parallel by suggesting that just as creators submit to the bent of their genius, so we appreciators submit to the cycle of anniversaries. To acknowledge ineluctable factors like birth and death is to ponder the mystery of creativity. Just as many creators thought of themselves as serving an impersonal force (which many call genius), consumers of culture must accept an impersonal cycle of anniversaries. Fundamental to the appeal of anniversaries is the realization that humans can do nothing to change some of the decisive events in their lives.

During the 1920s and 1930s existentialists like Martin Heidegger and Jean-Paul Sartre proclaimed the notion that no one chooses crucial factors in his life. In 1927 Heidegger introduced the concept of "thrownness" (*Geworfenheit*) to express the idea that each of us is thrown into the world at a time and in a place not of our choosing, indeed not of anyone's choosing.[5] Even if parents choose to have a child, they do not choose the temperament or gifts of the child born to them. Neither does the child select its parents; a child chooses neither the language nor the nation nor the religion nor the social status he inherits. None of the constraints that shape our start in life is chosen by us. The notion of thrownness states that none of us chooses where, when, or among whom we are tossed into existence.

During the 1940s and 1950s, particularly in France and Germany, existential philosophy offered consolation to generations that were rebuilding the ruins of World War II. Even though today existentialism seems either too heroic or too bleak to suit postmoderns, the notion of thrownness has largely replaced the idea that God nurtures a plan for every individual who comes into the world. For a majority of Europeans, if not of Americans, the notion of thrownness has supplanted the notion of God's Providence. What both ideas have in common is acknowledgment that humans do not govern crucial factors in their lives. Whether we say that God placed us in our situation or that we were thrown into it, the realization is the same: we did not select the timing or circumstances of our birth.

The cult of anniversaries is a secular device for inculcating this truth. By commemorating anniversaries in all their arbitrariness, we get reminded that no one, not even the greatest geniuses, selects the moment or manner of birth or death. Geniuses must submit to the same kind of thrownness as the rest of us. What we celebrate during the anniversary of a creator is a triumph over thrownness. Although no one chooses when or to whom to be born, many choose how to exercise creativity. Moreover, just as great creators assert their identity through the media of literature, art, music, or thought, so we appreciators assert ours through the medium of anniversaries. We triumph over our own thrownness by joining together to celebrate the triumph of others over theirs.

As luck would have it, two joint anniversaries of English writers during 1990 offer an opportunity to reflect on the interaction of choice with fatedness. The novelist Thomas Hardy (1840–1928) and the churchman John Henry Cardinal Newman (1801–1890) spent much of their adult lives wrestling with the consequences of fateful choices.

A joint commemoration of these two Victorians would have helped to illuminate the existential basis for the cult of anniversaries. In life as well as in doctrine, both men articulated very different conceptions of how fate shapes human lives.

Newman felt obliged to change allegiance from the Church of England to the Roman Catholic church, even though many leaders of the latter never welcomed him and leaders of the former shunned him. Hardy wrote upwards of ten novels about how minute mischances frustrate human aspirations, especially in courtship. He enlarged the concept of thrownness beyond the ambit of birth to include mischances that occur throughout life. For Hardy, thrownness meant not only being born into an unchosen role but having obstacles continually bedevil one in unforeseen ways. Newman, on the other hand, with his faith in God's Providence, believed that we can exercise meaningful choice by acknowledging dependence on God. Newman felt forced by God to choose the Roman Catholic church at a time when most churchmen deplored his choice. Throughout his career he taught that we can overcome the limitations of our original thrownness by trusting God to guide us into a path where thrownness turns into blessing. Both Hardy and Newman emphasized the challenge of obstacles thrown across our path, but they interpreted these obstacles in utterly different ways.

During 1990 a conference on "Concepts of Thrownness and Choice in Hardy and Newman" could have served to highlight ways in which the cult of anniversaries incorporates the notion of thrownness. What links the cycle of anniversaries to the experience of thrownness is the fact that we do not choose a given year's celebrands. The cycle of births and deaths throws them at us. Even if we choose which celebrands to emphasize, or how and where to commemorate them, we do not choose the year in which to do so. The cult of anniversaries requires us to acknowledge this reality. Whether we complain like Hardy or rejoice like Newman, the schema of anniversaries steers us without our having designed it.

Devotees of cultural anniversaries affirm that even if there is no God to sanction ritual, nevertheless we need rituals to remind us of the arbitrariness, or if you prefer the thrownness, of our condition. It is healthy to acknowledge thrownness, Europeans believe, and the cult of anniversaries allows a secular society to do so in unison. In Europe today major anniversaries command wider attention than do any religious observances. They focus admiration on figures worthy of it, and in so doing they remind everyone that no human being chooses when to be born or when to die. Whether one prefers the bitterness of Hardy or the joyfulness of Newman, anniversaries recall the eruption of the fortuitous into even the most carefully planned lives.

Indeed, the interaction of the fortuitous and the planned underpins the appeal of anniversaries. The dependence of programmers on the calendar may be said to mirror the dependence of creators on forces beyond their control. Programmers choose the days but not the years in which to commemorate creators, just as creators choose the means but not the ultimate realization of their creations. By welcoming a timing that no one chose, planners of anniversaries experience the kind of creative submission which celebrands too endured and which we in turn commemorate.

Submission to the cult of anniversaries thus invokes a Romantic notion of creativity, one that Europeans embrace more readily than do Americans. Most Europeans still expect inspiration to blow where it wills, while in the wake of the Enlightenment Americans prefer to emphasize teamwork, bureaucracy, and scheduling as spurs to innovation. In defiance of American assumptions, the cult of anniversaries declares that supreme inspiration cannot be scheduled. In a world increasingly dominated by timetables, the cult of anniversaries honors older modes of creativity. The cult of anniversaries allows planners to combine Enlightenment faith in schedules with romantic trust in inspiration. It plans moments in which to applaud unplanned eruptions of genius, something that both Hardy and Newman would have approved.

The Quest for Cycles across the Centuries

Any system of timekeeping involves imposing regularity on the linear flow of days, months, and years. As time moves onward, humans need to impose patterns upon it, and anniversaries supply a means of doing so. The sociologist Eviatar Zerubavel has done as much as anyone to examine how calendric rhythms enhance daily life, and his findings help to explain the appeal of anniversaries. He emphasizes the need to impose recurring patterns on the linear flow of time, arguing that cycles like that of the seven-day week bring reassurance simply by recurring. If there were no built-in routine, Zerubavel shows, people would suffer a deficit of regularity. He contends further that the need for cycles is not primarily religious, as scholars like Mircea Eliade have argued, but answers rather a psychological and social need for rhythmic alternations.[6] An ever-repeating seven-day week allows ordinary days to alternate with extraordinary ones. The cycle of weeks guarantees not boredom but rather an alternation of boredom with periods of peak activity. The need for recurrence cuts so deep that Zerubavel coined the term *homo rhythmicus* to proclaim this human proclivity.[7]

The concept of *homo rhythmicus* stresses the appeal of repetition in precise multiples, whether of days, months, or years. Humans impart meaning to the forward surge of time by living within weekly, monthly, and yearly rhythms. Annual holidays like Christmas and the Fourth of July illustrate the latter, while clubs that meet once a week or once a month illustrate the former. Historical anniversaries, it can be seen, furnish rhythms across not months or years, but centuries. Historical anniversaries impose circularity on longer spans of time, answering the need felt by *homo rhythmicus* for patterns that recur. The cult of anniversaries meets the need to experience repeatability on a large scale.

The media of mass culture have exploited this need by contriving anniversaries of events at a distance of as little as five and ten years. In 1988 and 1989 media in the United States commemorated the twentieth anniversary of various events of the 1960s including the Woodstock Festival of 1969. The flurry caused in 1989 by the twenty-fifth anniversary of the Beatles' arrival in the United States typifies mass culture's proliferation of short-range anniversaries. Preoccupation with events no more than a generation old shows how mass media tend to shorten the span of memory.

Historical anniversaries satisfy the need for recurrence across a longer span. To know that the French Revolution, World War I, and the American Civil War will be commemorated every fifty years imparts order to the unrolling of the years. Moreover, anniversaries of major events in the founding of a nation make those years "extraordinary" in just the way that the sabbath stands out within the week. Anniversaries of founding events become years to anticipate and to look back upon. For people whose cities commemorate a founding event, like the 750th of Berlin in 1987 or the 2000th of Strasbourg in 1988 or the 2000th of Bonn in 1989, those years will stand out across a decade and perhaps a lifetime.

Regularity of celebrations at fifty-year intervals means, moreover, that slightly over half those involved can hope to experience two such anniversaries, at say age twenty-five and seventy-five, while the other half will experience just one, somewhere between age thirty-five and fifty-five. Major anniversaries end in an acknowledgment: "We will not be doing this again for fifty years." Such attention to long-term rhythms cannot help but inspire reflection on human mortality. One purpose of commemorating a 500th or 2000th anniversary is to dramatize the reality that institutions endure but individuals do not.

The cult of anniversaries has proliferated during the 1980s partly because in an era that has largely abandoned any religious calendar, people crave comparable rhythms of a secular sort. If *homo rhythmicus* no longer attends weekly worship, he needs other reminders of recurring patterns. Historical anniversaries meet a need both psychological and social for humans to notch their identity into the calendar. National anniversaries assure citizens that their country and region matter in the flow of time. When inhabitants of a city or country declare certain years to be theirs, they affirm particularity not only in space but in time.

The Great Calendar and Its Secularization

A calendar represents a triumph of computation over chaos. Calendars impose cyclical order on what would otherwise be meaningless sequence. Just as the cycle of weeks imparts order to the work-a-day world, so the cycle of anniversaries imparts order to the march of centuries. Taking the longest view, what can be called the Great Calendar bundles years into centuries, centuries into millennia, and millennia into geological epochs, without regard to human chronology. The Great Calendar incorporates all the centuries since human beings in the ancient Middle East began to reckon time, and connects these with all the millennia since life began on earth. The Great Calendar is an abstraction that functions without reference to a single culture or starting point. First envisioned in the seventeenth century, it transcends all specific modes of reckoning time.

The cult of anniversaries in Europe and the United States builds upon Western civilization's particular mode of chronology. It is sobering to realize that calendars are one of humanity's more recent inventions. Innovations still more crucial for the rise of civilization like the taming of fire, the development of agriculture, and the introduction of weaving and potting evolved before calendars did. Taking such recent milestones in stride, the Great Calendar registers human accomplishments across hundreds of millennia from the earliest anthropoids to the present.

Our present-day version of the Great Calendar, known as the Gregorian calendar, derives from that of the ancient Romans, specifically from a reform that Julius Caesar introduced in 46 B.C.[8] His calendar calculated the length of time that it takes the earth to revolve around the sun as being 365 and one-quarter days. The Julian calendar regulated leap year (in order to allow for that extra quarter day), adjusted the names of the months (two of which were later altered to honor himself in July and his successor Augustus in August), and ratified the counting of years from the hypothetical founding of the city of Rome in a year that we now designate as 753 B.C.

The Julian calendar, with names for the months that we still use, remained in force in Catholic Europe for more than sixteen hundred years. In 1582 it was revised by a commission appointed by Pope Gregory XIII. Vatican astronomers, using an observatory that can still be visited, calculated that an error in Caesar's reckoning of leap year had allowed eleven extra days to accumulate since 46 B.C. These eleven days, caused by Caesar's overestimate of the length of each year, were dropped during the month of October 1582, and to prevent a repetition, leap year has been omitted thereafter during three out of every four turns-of-the-century. Remaining stubbornly anti-Catholic, the Protestant regions of Germany, Holland, and Switzerland, together with England and its American colonies, refused to adopt this necessary correction until the year 1752.[9] Even more defiantly, the Eastern Orthodox church in Russia, Greece, and Serbia retained the old style until the twentieth century. Moreover, the Gregorian calendar remained exclusively European until Japan adopted it in 1873, followed by Egypt in 1875. As Europeans conquered the rest of the globe, they brought the Western calendar to it, so that the entire world now regulates finance, airline schedules, and other forms of international interaction according to the Gregorian calendar. Surprisingly, in 1982 the 400th anniversary of its inception passed largely unnoticed.

The notion of absolute time as an abstraction that transcends any one culture's system of reckoning originated only in the seventeenth century. As envisioned by Isaac Newton, who spent forty years perfecting his idiosyncratic *Chronology of Ancient Kingdoms Amended* (1728), absolute time meant duration that unfolds without reference to anything external.[10] We concretize this temporal continuum by postulating a Great Calendar, better known as the Perpetual Calendar, which unrolls through the centuries without reference to any culture's calculations. Computations concerning it are based on the time of 365.242 days that is required for the earth to revolve in orbit around the sun. This unit is built into the structure of the solar system, as is the elapse of 29.535 days that it takes the moon to revolve around the earth.

Each major culture develops a version of the Great Calendar by numbering the revolutions of the earth around the sun (or as in the case of Islam, of revolutions of the moon around the earth) with reference to an arbitrary starting point. The ancient Jews reckoned from the creation of the earth in 3761 B.C. The ancient Greeks reckoned from the founding of the Olympic games in 776 B.C., while the ancient Romans calculated from the founding of their city in 753 B.C. Muslims proceed from the Hegira of Mohammed in July 622, using lunar years that alternate between 354 and 355 days.

Considering its present-day ubiquity, a chronology that reckons the Christian Era from the birth of Christ in A.D. 1 developed surprisingly late. It was first proposed in 525 by a Scythian monk living in Rome, Dionysius Exiguus (c. 500–550), who while computing Easter dates assigned the birth of Christ to March 25 of the year 1, that is to say, 753 years after the founding of Rome.[11] More than a century elapsed before the Synod of Whitby, meeting in England in 664 to settle disputes about the dating of Easter, adopted Dionysius's notion of the "Year of Our Lord" (*Anno Domini*), which Anglo-Saxon monks carried soon thereafter to the Continent. We now know that Dionysius Exiguus assigned the birth three or four years later than it actually occurred. Christ was born in 4 or 3 B.C. or perhaps a bit earlier, a discrepancy that is almost never heeded in planning Christian anniversaries.

Although as early as A.D. 700 the Christian church could have demarcated the Great Calendar by reference to the birth of Christ, use of the B.C./A.D. dating system emerged only in the mid-seventeenth century. A French Jesuit named Domenicus Petavius (1583–1652) proposed this convention in his *Opus de doctrina temporum* (1627), thereby replacing a myriad of relativistic systems that had come and gone for more than two thousand years.[12] Petavius's innovation located European history within the Great Calendar, in effect christianizing chronology. Few people then or now cared that the Christian calendar omits the year zero between 1 B.C. and A.D. 1. This omission complicates the calculation of anniversaries from the ancient world by making them fall a year later than common sense expects.

It broadens one's perspective to realize that any system of reckoning that commands universal assent would work equally well. As Petavius recognized, we could adopt a starting point any number of years ago, either 1000, 3000, 10,000, or any other total, provided everyone accepts the same point. This is another way of saying that calendars rely on convention, often invoking a sacred origin. Every society must impose a convention for reckoning dates, and once that convention takes root, no society will willingly alter it. The Jacobin revolutionaries in France learned this to their chagrin when the French public disdained the Revolutionary calendar, which in November 1793 was decreed to date from the fall equinox of 1792. Poetic verve could not save the new calendar from falling into disuse long before Napoleon abolished it at the end of 1805.[13] Similarly, during the 1930s Italians refused to abide by the Fascist calendar, which dated from the year 1922. Few things about a civilization endure longer than its system of reckoning dates.

The cult of anniversaries incorporates the notion of the Christian Era. Dionysius Exiguus and Domenicus Petavius together may be said to have shaped our cult of anniversaries, since working eleven hundred years apart they devised the system whereby we count centuries. Inevitably, the Christian origin of our system of dating raises an issue for secularists. Should they lobby to modify the Christian system of counting the years?[14] The Jacobins of the French Revolution tried and failed to substitute a secular calendar, which abolished saints' days as well as the sabbath. Having learned from the Jacobins' fiasco, the Soviet Revolution introduced the new style of the Gregorian calendar but did not inaugurate a socialist way of counting years. Because calendars require 100 percent adhesion, secularizers are wise not to challenge the existing framework.

They have concentrated instead on replacing Christian anniversaries with secular ones, for the cult of anniversaries provides a way to secularize the Christian calendar without jettisoning it. As public allegiance has shifted over the past two centuries from saints to creators, saints' days have given way to creators' anniversaries. Insofar as cultural managers can pack each year with secular commemorations, attention will shift, as it already has, from religious anniversaries to secular ones. Of late, the proliferation of secular anniversaries has eclipsed religious ones. The year of the 1500th anniversary of the birth of Saint Benedict in 1980 was known to most educated Europeans rather as the year of the artists Palladio, Bernini, and Ingres, the writers George Eliot and Robert Musil, and the Austrian rulers Maria Theresia and her son Joseph II. Similarly, the year of the 800th anniversary of Saint Francis in 1982 was celebrated by many instead as the year of the painter Claude Lorrain, the composer Franz Joseph Haydn, the scientist Charles Darwin, and the writers Virginia Woolf and James Joyce. Many cultivated Europeans savor secular anniversaries without ever noticing religious ones. That is one reason why historians increasingly call the Christian Era the Common Era.

As these examples show, every year throws up enough European luminaries to enthrall people of every vocation, interest, and nationality. Programmers need not deliberately substitute secular figures for saints, because no such Voltairean conspiracy is required. Secular commemorations abound because fascination with anniversaries of creators coincides with the availability of budgets to finance them. From around A.D. 50 until at least 1600 the countries of Europe fostered a galaxy of saints. Starting in the fourteenth century, the same countries fostered more and more secular creators, until by the seventeenth century, if not before, secular notables began to outnumber religious ones. National ministries of culture show a vested interest in commemorating secular figures with whom their citizens share a sense of identity.

Secular creators who have flourished since the sixteenth century account for an overwhelming majority of Europe's cultural commemorations. Indeed, part of what Europeans commemorate each year is emergence from under the tutelage of the Church. Nowadays at least three-fourths of the anniversaries celebrated in Britain, France, Germany, and Austria commemorate secular figures who have thrived since 1750. It is the bringers of enlightenment, or modernity, who each year get the most fanfare. By favoring enlighteners or modernizers, cultural programmers publicize the triumph of the Enlightenment over the Old Regime (from before 1789) as well as over the Protestant and Catholic churches that supported it. Such secular triumphalism ran riot during the Bicentennial of the French Revolution. Through the cult of anniversaries, Europeans celebrate their emancipation from the Old Regime with even more zeal than Americans celebrate their independence from Britain. To be sure, in allocating resources between church and state, Germany and Austria (as well as Alsace) represent an anomaly because priests there still draw subsidies from cultural ministries. In countries where state taxes still finance the clergy, cultural managers can subvert this anachronism by commemorating figures who championed secularism.

These nuances of cultural life in Western Europe suggest further reasons why the cult of anniversaries flourishes there. Not only does it situate *homo rhythmicus* within the Great Calendar and remind people of the ineluctable in life, but it allows secularists to campaign against Christianity. The cult of anniversaries is not merely a convenience for schedulers, but also a weapon for advancing their goals. The next chapter examines how cultural ministries in Europe and local organizers in the United States exploit anniversaries in order to promote national and regional identity.

Notes

1. R.R. Palmer, *The Improvement of Humanity: Education and the French Revolution* (Princeton: Princeton University Press, 1985); Emmet Kennedy, *A Cultural History of the French Revolution* (New Haven: Yale University Press, 1989), pp. 155–167.
2. Jean Lacouture, *Malraux: Une vie dans le siècle* (Paris: Seuil, 1973), translated as *André Malraux* (New York: Pantheon, 1975), chap. 38; William M. Johnston, "Europas Museen reimaginiert: Variationen über ein Thema André Malraux," in Peter Noever, ed., *Tradition und Experiment: Das Österreichische Museum für angewandte Kunst, Wien* (Salzburg: Residenz Verlag, 1989), pp. 255–265.
3. James R. Beniger, *The Control Revolution: Technological and Economic Origins of the Information Society* (Cambridge: Harvard University Press, 1986) traces the emergence of control mechanisms.
4. English festivals celebrating French music included those at Brighton, Greenwich, Cheltenham, Cambridge, Buxton, Edinburgh, Warwick, Norfolk, and Norwich. See Vernon Kidd, "Echoes of the Revolution," *New York Times* (April 30, 1989), sec. 5, p. 18. On commemorative aspects of music festivals, see Percy M. Young, "Festivals," in *The New Grove*

Dictionary of Music and Musicians (New York: Macmillan, 1980), 6: 505–510; includes extensive bibliography.

5. Martin Heidegger, "Das Verfallen und die Geworfenheit," in *Sein und Zeit* (Halle a.d., 1927); translated as *Being and Time*, John Macquarrie and Edward Robinson, trans. (London: SCM Press, 1962).

6. Eviatar Zerubavel, *The Seven Day Circle: The History and Meaning of the Week* (New York: Free Press, 1985), p. 85.

7. Eviatar Zerubavel, *Hidden Rhythms: Schedules and Calendars in Social Life* (Chicago: University of Chicago Press, 1981).

8. Giulia Piccaluga, "Calendars: An Overview," *Encyclopedia of Religion*, 3 (1987); 7–11, states major issues in the comparative study of calendars. Zerubavel, *The Seven Day Circle*, pp. 60–82, examines what he calls the "harmonics of timekeeping," that is, the mathematical difficulties of coordinating 7-day weeks with 30-day months and 365-day years. See also Zerubavel, *Hidden Rhythms*, pp. 70–100.

9. Zerubavel, *Hidden Rhythms*, pp. 99–100.

10. Donald J. Wilcox, *The Measure of Times Past: Pre-Newtonian Chronology and the Rhetoric of Relative Time* (Chicago: University of Chicago Press, 1987), pp. 22–23, 208–214.

11. Wilcox, *The Measure of Times Past*, pp. 137–138.

12. Wilcox, *The Measure of Times Past*, pp. 8, 203–208.

13. Zerubavel, *The Seven Day Circle*, pp. 28–35; Mona Ozouf, "Revolutionary Calendar," in Furet and Ozouf, eds., *A Critical Dictionary of the French Revolution* (Cambridge: Harvard University Press, 1989), pp. 538–547.

14. See Hannah Arendt, "The Concept of History," in *Between Past and Future: Eight Exercises in Political Thought* (New York: Viking, 1969), pp. 63–68 on this and other consequences of adopting a Christian mode of reckoning time.

3

National Identity and Its Propagation
through Anniversaries

National Identity in Europe and Its Appeal to Intellectuals

The cult of anniversaries helps cultural programmers to achieve consensus, and it helps everyone to get situated within the Great Calendar of history. Equally important, the cult of anniversaries helps governments and businesses to cultivate national identity. The notion of national identity underlies the appeal of cultural anniversaries, as much in the United States as in Europe. What is national identity and how does it function in individual countries? How do anniversaries help governments to promote it? This chapter examines Europe's reliance on cultural anniversaries as a device for propagating national identity, and then explores reasons why the United States construes anniversaries differently.

As the countries of Western Europe have integrated their economies since the 1950s, each nation has needed more urgently than before to proclaim a sense of distinctiveness. A shared sense of distinctiveness, as it has unfolded in a nation-state's history, is what is called a national identity. National identity is a form of consciousness, consciousness of belonging to a nation-state that knows how to articulate its reasons for existing by invoking continuity between past and future. Publicists articulate national identity by connecting a nation's history with present-day endeavors. National identity has two aspects: it is at once a body of ideas that publicists elaborate, and it is an individual's absorption of those ideas into a personal identity.

In order to understand anniversaries, it is helpful to distinguish national identity from ethnic identity. The latter term means different things in Europe and in the United States. In Europe, ethnic identity refers to consciousness of belonging to a minority like the Bretons, the Welsh, or the Basques, who have not yet established a nation-state but some of whom would like to do so.[1] Before 1918 Austria-Hungary abounded in such ethnic minorities, most of whom succeeded in establishing a nation-state after World War I. The Soviet Union still includes many minorities who yearn for independence. In the United States, on the other hand, ethnic identity refers to consciousness of descent from either a national or ethnic group abroad. It does not imply, as it does in Europe, an aspiration to secede from the existing state.

Both in Europe and the United States, many people espouse both an ethnic identity and a national identity, not to mention regional and local identities as well. Most Europeans think of their identity as multiple, ascending in a hierarchy from town or city, through region or province, to culminate in the nation-state. An increasing number of Europeans now feel a transnational identity for "Europe" as well. A resident of Florence, for example, is at once Florentine, Tuscan, Italian, and European, just as a resident of Munich is Muenchner, Bavarian, German, and European. National identity is one of many levels of cultural identity, all of which get promoted through the cult of anniversaries.

Because national identity is so powerful in Europe, it is worth mentioning a country where national identity failed to crystallize. Argentina is a country of immigrants, which unlike the United States and Australia has failed to establish a national identity. In 1914, at a time when Argentina was one of the world's wealthiest countries and seemed poised to sever emotional ties to the Old World, too many of its residents (30 percent) were foreign-born to allow a sense of Argentinianness to develop.[2] Since then, Argentinians have continued to identify with their country of origin rather than with their adopted one. Australians, until the 1970s, had something of the same problem of overidentifying with a mother country, but their bicentennial in 1988 consummated a twenty-year process of consolidating national identity. Argentinians have not been so fortunate, and needless to say, have few anniversaries to commemorate.

National identity emerged as a potent force in Europe during the Early Modern period from 1500 to 1789. The monarchies of Spain,

France, and England, which during the Middle Ages had gathered feudal holdings into a royal domain and then into a nation-state, felt impelled to proclaim how each kingdom differed from the others. During the seventeenth and eighteenth centuries national identity got shaped largely through rejecting the counteridentity of rival nations.[3] British publicists, for example, denounced the France of the Bourbons, so that France's Catholic, absolutist, and centralized monarchy prodded the British to emphasize their Protestant, parliamentary, and decentralized character. During the eighteenth century Prussia invoked Austria as a counteridentity, and in the nineteenth century so did the Kingdom of Savoy in its endeavor to liberate Italy from Austria. The cult of anniversaries exalts writers like Shakespeare, Molière, and Schiller who played a role in defining either identities or counteridentities.

Why do writers, and particularly dramatists, play such a crucial role in shaping national identity? One reason is that nations build their self-image around a cluster of half-legendary ancestors who require writers and historians to bring them to life. Figures like Boadicea and King Alfred in Britain, Vercingetorix and King Clovis in France, Arminius and Charlemagne in Germany, among countless others, need to be imagined in order to compel loyalty. Writers who help us imagine ancestors play an indispensable role, because some of the honorees never existed or never belonged to the nation that appropriates them. The historical plays of Shakespeare, the operas of Wagner, and the tragedies of Racine furnish each country renewable images of those it takes for cultural ancestors. Italy, for example, commemorated the 200th anniversary of Alessandro Manzoni (1785–1873) with particular fervor, because his novel *The Betrothed* (1827; rev. ed., 1842) is one of the few that helps to define a national past. He ranks among the inventors of tradition in modern Italy, and as Eric Hobsbawm has shown, national tradition needs to be invented before it can be inherited.[4]

Not just delineators of history but all writers and artists play a further role in the invention of tradition by getting incorporated into it. Insofar as a nation must be imagined before it can be experienced, writers and artists themselves come to occupy the imaginary space that a sense of nationhood evokes.[5] Cultivated Europeans learn in school to identify with certain creators whose accomplishments comprise the national heritage. Goethe and Schiller in Germany, Montaigne and Racine in France, Dante and Michelangelo in Italy, Chaucer and Milton in England among innumerable others embody national identity in ways that nourish imagination. The inventors of tradition become part of what they invented, and naturally their anniversaries command special attention.

Peoples who chafe under empires that block them from forming nation-states cultivate not national identity but its predecessor, national character. Any national identity requires acts of imagination, but national character consists of nothing else. The latter is a notion that blossomed during the Romantic era, particularly among the subject peoples of the Hapsburg Empire, who relied all the more on imagination because they had no nation state to call their own.[6] Throughout the nineteenth century peoples like the Czechs, Hungarians, Poles, and Slovenes articulated a sense of identity by glorifying heroes, reviving vernacular languages, and evoking ancestral traits. This is what the Bretons in France, the Welsh in Britain, and the Basques in Spain, not to mention nationalities in the Soviet Union, still do today. National character, as distinct from national identity, may be defined as consciousness of unfulfilled nationhood conveyed almost exclusively through literary and artistic models. Literature matters most where no state institutions exist to transmit it.

Among peoples aspiring to forge a nation-state, the Germans of the early and mid-nineteenth century pioneered the use of cultural anniversaries to focus their imaginings. The Wartburgfest held in 1817 on the 300th anniversary of Martin Luther's Ninety-five Theses, together with the centennial of the birth of Friedrich Schiller in 1859, did much to awaken German national consciousness. As we shall see in Chapter 5, aspirations for German nationhood provided a principal source for the cult of anniversaries.

The other major source was the celebrations that accompanied the French Revolution during the 1790s. Already on July 14, 1790, the French celebrated the first anniversary of the fall of the Bastille. On August 10, 1793, they "commemorated" the first anniversary of the overthrow of monarchy by disembowelling the tombs of previous kings in the Abbey of Saint-Denis. From the start of the Revolution, the French invoked anniversaries to commemorate an achieved sense of nationhood, while the Germans used them to advocate creation of a nation. To this day, German cultural anniversaries tend to construe nationhood as something yet to be completed, while French ones exude a sense of consummation. During the early 1990s, as Germany unifies for the second time in a century and a quarter, this difference will intensify.

Not only is the national identity of the French older and firmer than that of the Germans or Italians, but it also incorporates an ingredient of cosmopolitanism. During the seventeenth and eighteenth centuries French prevailed as the language of courts, diplomacy, and international culture throughout Europe. *Philosophes* like Voltaire and Diderot, who sojourned at the courts of Prussia and Russia, embodied France's image as a nation whose culture transcends its borders. As Thomas Jefferson is said to have put it, "Every man has two countries, his own and France." Inevitably, French identity involves a mission to spread the values of French culture to other nations. The "civilizing mission" of the French flowered during the eighteenth century, triumphed throughout the Revolutionary and Napoleonic periods, and got renewed under Louis-Philippe and Napoleon III in the mid-nineteenth century. As a result, the French feel no surprise that countries as diverse as Spain and Russia or the Netherlands and Italy adopted and retained French inventions like the metric system, the rhetoric of revolution, and the Napoleonic law codes. The French crave expansion of their culture as a substitute for expanding their boundaries.

A need to articulate national identity came into its own following the French Revolution and the reign of Napoleon. The nineteenth century has been called the century of nationalism, when newly unified states like Belgium in 1830, Italy in 1860, and Germany in 1871 joined the established nation-states of Spain, France, and Britain. Resisting this trend, down to 1918 the Hapsburg Empire contained at least six potential nation-states, whose peoples sullenly waited. In 1918 and 1919 the Hapsburg territories were divided among seven nation-states, five of which were entirely new (Austria, Hungary, Czechoslovakia, Yugoslavia, and Poland). Of these five, Austria alone suffered an inadequate national identity because it derived from the Hapsburg Empire, yearning not for national identity but for a lost imperial one. Under the First Republic (1918–1938), Austria failed to solidify a national identity because too many Austrians wanted to be part of Germany. Consequently, since 1955 the Second Republic has had to rely unduly on cultural anniversaries to instil a sense of identity. In contrast to France or Britain, Austria today uses anniversaries not merely to cement but to formulate national identity.[7]

Since World War II the eighteen-odd nations of Western Europe have needed more than ever to proclaim national identity. After governments adopted expensive programs of social welfare in the 1950s, ministers had to persuade taxpayers to pay for the benefits. More recently, as Western Europe moves toward economic integration, each nation-state must justify continued independence in the face of beckoning unification. It is more vital than ever for France, let us say, to explain to its citizens why they are paying taxes to it and not to Germany or to Europe. The economic unification of Western Europe in 1993 will have the consequence of making each nation's cultural anniversaries more rather than less important. Moreover, because European countries operate a national school system, or as in the case of Germany a regional one, schools contrive to tell pupils why they study under national rather than international or municipal administration. History teachers must explain how their country's borders emerged, how its language grew, and how national and regional capitals arose. A country can further all of these tasks by commemorating anniversaries.

Besides international integration, another innovation that fosters anniversaries is state ownership of television. Because until very recently radio and television in Europe have functioned as a monopoly of the nation-state, managers have favored programs that articulate national identity. To do so, they rely unashamedly on the calendar of commemorations. Everyone knows that television tends to personalize the news.[8] It thrives by linking events to personalities with whom viewers can identify. Every year European television and radio produce films, plays, and interviews that bring that year's celebrands into the living room. State-run media cannot resist the temptation to exploit anniversary figures or events. During September 1989, for example, French, German, Italian, and British television showed many films about the start of World War II fifty years earlier. By imposing consensus, anniversaries fulfill a television programmer's dream. State subsidies follow the Great Calendar.

The situation differs in the United States. One reason that its cultural anniversaries (other than of popular culture) do not command a national audience is that American mass media are too commercial to heed them. In Europe, the entire cultural infrastructure, including the electronic media, school systems, universities, and museums, gets financed through national or regional authorities that seek to abet national or regional identity. In the United States, on the other hand, private broadcasters, local school boards, private universities, and independent museums find no comparable interest, either financial or bureaucratic, in proclaiming national identity.

American intellectuals who envy Europe its state financing of cultural initiatives can easily overlook a price this exacts, namely that the state requires recipients to address issues of national identity. By invoking consensus, the cult of anniversaries provides a conduit from national funding agencies to local organizers. Where all parties concur that an anniversary deserves commemorating, the funders do not care how it gets celebrated so long as the organizers acclaim the nationality of the celebrand. Anniversaries of canonical figures provide an opportunity for the state to channel money to towns, regions, and private bodies for the purpose of propagating local, regional, or national identity. To give some examples from German-speaking Europe, in 1982 the Austrian region of Styria mounted an exhibition and lectures to honor its modernizing prince Archduke Johann (1782–1859). On a vaster scale, in 1983 both the Federal Republic of Germany and the German Democratic Republic financed commemorations of the national hero Martin Luther (1483–1546). On a local level, in 1988 the German town of Konstanz commemorated the inventor of the dirigible, Graf von Zeppelin (1838–1917). In none of these cases did it matter to the funders what individual participants said about the celebrands, because the mere fact of publicizing them reinforced national identity.

The European cult of anniversaries presupposes state financing of cultural budgets. Schools, universities, theaters, museums, literary organizations, and cultural institutes abroad thrive on state funding. In return for investing in culture, state agencies expect these activities to enhance national identity. Intellectuals who get paid to organize and attend anniversary commemorations acquiesce in becoming retainers of the state. The device that more than any other eases such dependency is the cult of anniversaries. It mediates between the state's interest in promoting national identity and intellectuals' interest in playing a public role.

On anniversary occasions intellectuals get paid to discuss how a celebrand personified or challenged certain conceptions of national identity. In Europe such discussions take place every month at academic conferences, every week on television, and every day in the press.[9] This system of patronage works because a celebrand need not have been an ideologue in order to personify national identity. The mere fact of citizenship suffices to link a celebrand with the nation or locality that honors him. No one questions whether anniversaries of local and national heroes deserve to be celebrated or whether intellectuals should be paid to do so. A kind of Commonwealth of Anniversaries has emerged in present-day Europe, whereby intellectuals accept subsidies for articulating national values, even when they disagree with much of what is done in the name of those values.

Whereas in Europe national agencies promote cultural values, in the United States it is the private sector that sponsors cultural initiatives. By separating church and state, the American Constitution separated culture and state as well. As a result, American intellectuals hardly ever function as spokespersons for the national government, and many would decline to do so if asked. In Europe, by way of contrast, national funding of schools, universities, and electronic media make state and culture interdependent. In some countries national funding extends to churches as well. Napoleon in his Concordat of 1801 established the precedent that the state should pay the salaries of priests in exchange for state ownership of church land. This system lasted in France until 1905 (in Alsace it continues to the present), and a regional version of it endures in Germany and Austria.[10] If the state can subsidize priests as well as pay professors, then surely no intellectual will feel he has sold out by accepting fees from the state for casual appearances.

Until recently, not all intellectuals endorsed state financing of culture. During the nineteenth century in France, many avant-garde writers and artists spurned subsidies made available through prizes, salons, and court concerts. One reason the artistic avant-garde has disappeared in Europe since the 1960s is that hardly anyone any longer renounces state funding for literary or artistic endeavors. Today potential members of the avant-garde accept subsidies like everyone else. Since the demise of avant-gardes helped to usher in postmodernism, anniversaries have played a role in legitimating that shift. As we have seen, the cult of anniversaries provides a device to veil the dependence of creators on the state. Having imbibed at school texts by canonical writers, intellectuals delight in commemorating those ancestors. Every graduate of secondary school knows who are the iconic figures of his national literature and art, just as he knows that they will get commemorated throughout his life. Because in Europe encounter with these figures begins so young, the act of identifying with them, or of rebelling against them, evokes more intensity there than it can in the United States. School-leaving examinations burn exemplars of national identity into the memory, and intellectuals can spend their careers honoring favorites among these figures. The school system enlists recruits for the cult of anniversaries at an age before anyone dares to protest.

An intellectual can play the anniversary game equally successfully in support or dissent. An iconoclast, who denounces the claims of Victor Hugo or Friedrich Schiller or Alessandro Manzoni to monopolize attention during their anniversary years, will receive the same respect as one who extols national aims. State agencies do not demand a chorus of praise for celebrands, so long as attention cascades upon them. As with news media in general, the cult of anniversaries obeys the maxim: "The only bad publicity is no publicity." So long as celebrands get discussed, whether in praise or censure, sponsors achieve their goal of enhancing national identity. As orchestrated through anniversaries, national identity kindles a glow of self-congratulation in which Europeans bask. Cultural institutions get lubricated each year through a fresh roster of anniversaries, at which intellectuals dispute what is up-to-date and what is old-fashioned in the national and local identity of that year's crop.

Britain stands halfway between the Continent and the United States in its mode of funding cultural enterprises. Although England has a tradition of nationally endowed theater and at least since the 1870s of national schools, universities like Oxford and Cambridge are cantankerously independent. The Anglican church, moreover, with its endowments and other Trollopian strategems, resists homogenization. Traditions of eccentricity, sustained by the landed wealth of the aristocracy, the gentry, and the church, contribute to a spirit of defiance that refuses to identify the nation with its culture. To many Britons the Napoleonic notion of state-sponsored culture seems an impertinence. As a result, Britain more conspicuously than France or Germany purveys an image of national identity tailored to tourists rather than natives. For all these reasons, British intellectuals take commemorations of national identity less to heart than do their Continental counterparts. Intellectuals who discourse about anniversaries for the weekend newspapers or on television do so on their own behalf with scant regard to national identity.

There are additional reasons why British commemorations often seem contrived. The tradition of two-party government makes any exploitation of an anniversary by the party in power suspect to the opposition. During 1988, for example, celebrations of the 400th anniversary of the Spanish Armada or the 300th of the Glorious Revolution lacked national consensus. Critics of Margaret Thatcher's government dismissed these enterprises as confections designed to enhance the prestige not so much of Britain as of its Conservative government. Attempts to promote municipal identity fared no better. During 1989 Britain's second largest city, Birmingham, scheduled more than seven hundred events to commemorate its elevation to the status of city in 1889. As befitted a manufacturing community better known for commerce than elegance, the centennial sponsored a bewildering assortment of activities ranging from canal rides to a jazz festival. Hardly anyone outside of the British Midlands noticed this celebration of urban infrastructure. Similarly, during July 1989 a celebration in London of the 800th anniversary of the office of Lord Mayor produced a standard mix of events, including a visit of Tall Ships, guided walks, and a party on London Bridge. No one seemed to care that the same Tall Ships would pay a visit a few weeks later to Hamburg Harbor to mark its 800th anniversary. Britain is not the only country in which anniversaries of governmental bodies tap no depth of feeling.

To make matters worse, the monarchy eclipses such endeavors, whether national or local, by competing for attention. Since the monarchy is presumed to embody national identity, its anniversaries are almost the only ones that rise above party. A typical British anniversary is the celebration of Royal Oak Day on May 29 to mark Charles II's founding in 1682 of the Royal Hospital for retired soldiers in Chelsea. These annual festivities emphasize the royal founder of the hospital, thereby honoring through him the nation his pensioners served. Whether for good or ill, the royal family scarcely wishes to promote anniversaries of writers, artists, or musicians. Consequently, as in the United States, the initiative for creators' anniversaries passes by default to universities and cultural associations, who generally lack funds to undertake anything spectacular.

Competing Interpretations of the French Revolution
and Postmodern Discourse

Government sponsorship threatens to taint European commemorations with party propaganda, or so outsiders tend to believe. In point of fact, this hardly ever happens because Western European cultural ministries invite every possible interpretation to get aired. Increasingly, anniversary commemorations resemble world's fairs at which all contenders hawk their wares. When sponsoring commemorations, the state functions as facilitator rather than propagandist, secure in the knowledge that discussion of any sort will enhance national identity.

The most remarkable recent example of a world's fair of interpretations has been the bicentennial of the French Revolution. It was inconceivable that the French government could evade commemorating this anniversary. Rather than push the onus of sponsoring conflicting interpretations onto private bodies or local governments as would have happened in the United States, the French state shouldered the task with alacrity, both at home and abroad. Moreover, a once-in-a-lifetime political alignment made the politics of the bicentennial more lively than anyone could have anticipated. The fact that the city of Paris was celebrating the bicentennial of its first mayor in 1789 meant that two bicentennials were conducted concurrently, that of the French Revolution and that of the autonomy of Paris. The national government, led by two Socialists, President François Mitterand and Prime Minister Michel Rocard, vied to outdo the administration of Paris, led by France's chief conservative politician, Mayor Jacques Chirac. Mitterand and Chirac reenacted in celebrating the Bicentennial the rivalry that had enlivened their term together in national government between 1986 and 1988. In sponsoring three major building projects that transform the east-west axis of Paris, Mitterand undoubtedly won the contest. The Opera at the Bastille, the Pyramid at the Louvre, and the Arch at the Place de la Défense will remain as memorials to the Bicentennial the way the Eiffel Tower remains from the Centennial of 1889. In tacit acknowledgment of this, at the climax of festivities in mid-July 1989 Mayor Chirac absented himself from the extravanganzas that President Mitterand hosted.

If anything threatened the impact of the Revolutionary bicentennial, it was not the intrusion of party propaganda, but rather the overabundance of interpretations. The bicentennial risked foundering under the weight of dozens of conferences, scores of exhibitions, hundreds of books, and thousands of popular events. A major film, *The Revolution,* nearly seven hours in length, competed with a locally financed one called *Vent de Galerne*, which dramatized the civil wars of 1793 in Western France. No one could digest even a quarter of what was offered. The very scope of the enterprise threatened its relevance to scholarship, allowing commercial considerations to outweigh scholarly ones. Paris became a marketplace of memorabilia, as hawkers of T-shirts, Phrygian bonnets, and printed ephemera haunted every bicentennial site. The cult of anniversaries has become a marketing device that meets the needs of all partakers at the feast of contemporary culture. Because no alternative commands a similar consensus, too many resources, both public and private, get committed to a commemoration like that of the French Revolution.

Anniversaries allow issues of high culture to enter the mainstream, exposing mass audiences to issues once reserved for an educated elite. By involving intellectuals with the mass media, commemorations encourage popularization. Seldom before during peacetime has European culture offered a forum of communication that meets the needs of so many so effectively as do anniversaries. The need of governments to cultivate public memory coincides with the ambition of writers, curators, advertisers, and media people to share the limelight. The ministries that finance all this bask in reflected glory, while scholars enjoy a few hours or days of celebrity.

Academic historians may resent the fact that their monopoly on study of the French Revolution has crumbled. From now on, most individuals will associate the Revolution not with the Tennis Court Oath of June 1789 or the March on Versailles of October 1789 but rather with the extravanganzas that Mitterand's France and Chirac's Paris mounted to commemorate these and other events. Reenactments, films, and exhibitions, not to mention kitsch memorabilia, have preempted all previous images. At the Tuileries Gardens during 1989 androids, comic strips, and computer simulations competed as media for visualizing the events of 1789. Bicentennial imagery will so completely displace previous interpretations that hereafter it will be difficult to disentangle the French Revolution from the myriad replays of it confected during 1989. To take one example among many, a tricolor flag 200 feet long painted on the cliffs above the Norman town of Le Tréport will not soon fade from local memory.

The image of the French Revolution has been postmodernized under state supervision. In France, which abounds in state-run enterprises, the bicentennial became a gigantic state enterprise, in which the government at all levels undertook to heighten public perceptions of a pivotal event. In keeping with the axiom that any publicity about a nation's past promotes national identity, it did not matter whether a citizen accepted or rejected any of the current interpretations of the Revolution, so long as he associated them with the French state. Although most French people professed to be bored by the bicentennial, the organizers could deem it a success because it forced everyone to assess French national identity. The emergence of counterbicentennials, which focused on the Third World and on victims of the guillotine, only enhanced the overall impact.

Mitterand's Socialists and Chirac's Conservatives launched a kind of *cohabitation* to commemorate the bicentennial, and such collaboration accords with the postmodern habit of hedging intellectual bets. No dominant interpretation can emerge, as it did in 1889, when the Great Revolution served to legitimate the institutions of the Third Republic.[11] Instead, fashioners of composites splice together bits of previous interpretations. The postbicentennial image, multiple and shifting, will be a quilt of conflicting views, which share the grandeur and misery of having flowered during the commemorative year.

Interpretations presented in hundreds of venues can be compared to the offerings at national pavilions of a world's fair. Consumers will remember the new contentions as being products of the universal exposition of the Revolutionary bicentennial, where even the most farfetched interpretations can subsist if only as sideshows. Commemorative fanfare will supplant the original event in people's minds, so that during the 1990s people will recall not the events of 1789 but of their repackaging in 1989. Commemoration has all but superseded less manipulative forms of collective memory.

The prospect of losing sight of original events need not alarm postmoderns. Because most scholars have long since abandoned Leopold von Ranke's notion that anyone can know the Revolution as it really was, the German historian's ghost no longer haunts professionals.[12] Experts accept the fact that interpretations will multiply without any hope of reducing them to consensus. Even if a few cling to Rankian aspirations of recapturing the past "as it really was," their demand for evidence goes unmet. The Rankian notion of historical verifiability has become just one among many criteria of discourse. One reason that anniversaries flourish is that they offer a way to convey the past to a public that no longer believes in the possibility of knowing it authoritatively.

Civil Religion and Its Varieties in Europe

The French Revolution reinforced national identity not least by introducing a civil religion to justify the new regime. Starting in the 1780s successive countries had to invent what Rousseau called a civil religion whenever the type of government evolved from monarchy to republic. Designed to divert sacred values onto the state, a civil religion may be defined as "the religious or quasi-religious regard for certain civic values and traditions found recurrently in the history of the political state."[13] Newly founded republics, starting with the United States in 1787 and France in 1792, needed to channel loyalty away from a monarchy onto a new regime. One way to do so was to introduce rituals that would siphon loyalty from the existing churches onto the republic. Some of the differences in the use of anniversaries among European nations today go back to the type of civil religion that they adopted.

Under France's First Republic in 1792 and 1793, Robespierre inaugurated a civil religion consisting of festivals, revolutionary anniversaries, a new calendar, and deism in the guise of worship of the Supreme Being.[14] This civil religion aimed not only to supplant Christianity but to mark the beginning of a new era. Although the Jacobin festivals soon withered and the new calendar never won popularity, a tradition of venerating revolution has endured to this day. France's civil religion exalts the cult of the French Revolution. Since the revolutionaries invented the political use of anniversaries when they celebrated the first anniversary of the Fall of the Bastille, it was only natural for the Third Republic ninety years later to declare July 14 as the national holiday. They did so in 1880 on the ninetieth anniversary not of the event itself but of its first commemoration.[15] In so doing the Third Republic was commemorating the cult of commemorations that its predecessor had invented.[16] Although political and cultural anniversaries fit organically into the civil religion of revolutionary France, fewer and fewer French people take this religion seriously. The malaise occasioned by the grandiosity of the bicentennial in 1989 stemmed not least from the decay of civil religion. Commercialism has driven out quasi-religious fervor.

In newly unified Germany, a civil religion emerged in the 1870s in the form of secularized courtly rituals like the Bayreuth festival of Wagner's operas as well as the celebration of military victories. In 1913, for example, the centennial of the defeat of Napoleon at Leipzig occasioned the erection of a huge monument there as well as of a Russian Orthodox church to commemorate the allies of 1813. For the educated middle classes, however, German national identity after 1870 rested not on a civil religion of the new state but rather on older traditions of theater, art, and literature such as Goethe and Schiller had personified at Weimar in the later eighteenth century. These Weimar classicists inspired a civil religion of *Kultur,* which to this day stresses the anniversaries of creators, particularly writers and musicians.

Because Weimar's leaders were secular, this civil religion owed little to either Catholicism or Protestantism. It was a cult rather of humanist creativity that tended toward secularism. In sinister fashion, the Nazis debased Germany's civil religion of culture by elaborating Wagnerian stagecraft into quasi-pagan rituals that strove to supplant both Christianity and Weimar classicism. Nazi imposition of a semi-pagan civil religion discredited any but the most apolitical civil religion in post-1945 West Germany. Nazi abuses also weakened the appeal of Christianity in post-1945 Europe, where many people cannot yet forgive the church for failing to resist crimes committed in the name of a totalitarian civil religion.

As a result of these traumas, the cult of anniversaries in West Germany has shown a distinctly nonpartisan and nonreligious character. In the absence of a civil religion of the state, cultural luminaries receive disproportionate attention. West German cultural commemorations, many of them funded by the regions (*Länder*), revived the apolitical quality of pre-1848 Biedermeier Germany. A preference has emerged for honoring apolitical figures, as happened in 1988 for the poet Joseph von Eichendorff (1788–1857) and the philosopher Arthur Schopenhauer (1788–1860), both of whom opted out of the political arena. Anniversaries of artists, philosophers, musicians, and writers has displaced any other civil religion in West Germany. These occasions reknit ties with a Biedermeier tradition, just as those of France do with a revolutionary one. Germany's civil religion smacks of Biedermeier passivity, as people recoil from more recent memories. The unification of Germany will probably enhance these trends, at least for a while, as Germans strive to allay their neighbors' fears of hegemony.

The situation is more complicated in Austria because the Republic of Austria did not succeed in cementing a national identity until the 1980s. Austria may be the only European country whose national identity matured during the present Age of Anniversaries. Since 1955 the identity of Austria's Second Republic has rested on three very different pillars: nostalgia for the culture promoted by the Hapsburg court between 1300 and 1918, memories of ties before 1918 to other regions of the Danube Basin (particularly Hungary), and aversion to the Nazi state, which ruled Austria from 1938 to 1945. Austria's civil religion of Hapsburg memories focuses on the imperial capital of Vienna, where anniversaries from the Hapsburg era take on a republican twist. It is typical of postmodern Austria, for example, that socialist ministers affiliate themselves not only with princely composers like Haydn and Mozart but also with imperial rulers like Maria Theresia and Franz Joseph.

The ubiquity of music in Austria facilitates the use of anniversaries to solidify national identity. Just as this least verbal of art forms escaped police censorship during the early nineteenth century, so today it embellishes every sort of public occasion. It is no accident that for the bicentennial of Mozart's death in 1991 Austrian state television is sponsoring the largest project in the history of broadcasting: the filming of Mozart's entire output. Austria's civil religion consists most fundamentally of a cult of music and theater, in which the budget for the state theaters nearly exceeds that for the military. Waltzes, operettas, and schmaltzy songs, performed by state orchestras, provide continuity with popular entertainment of the nineteenth century. A cult of the theater imparts a tone of neutrality that suits the postmodern era in a country that fashioned its national identity only within the past twenty years.

National identity in Italy rests on a quite different foundation. The towns and regions of Italy developed such firm identities during the Middle Ages and the Renaissance that after the kingdom of Italy emerged in 1860, it struggled to overcome fierce local loyalties. Even today, many Italians feel closer to their city or their region than to the nation-state. Although the Fascists introduced a bogus civil religion that trumpeted ancient Roman symbols like the fasces, the wolf, and rotund architecture, it could not supplant Catholicism as the genuine civil religion of Italy. Most Italians, however secularized, retain a Catholic identity. Having been baptized as Catholics, they get married in the church and are buried from the church.

As a result, in no other European country except Spain are local identity and national identity so closely linked with anniversaries of saints as in Italy. Saint Francis, Saint Anthony of Padua, and Saint Catherine of Siena are national heroes, comparable to Luther in Germany or Napoleon in France, but probably even more popular. In June 1989 the Italian church celebrated the fiftieth anniversary of the proclamation of Saint Catherine of Siena as the Protrectress of Italy. In countless towns, particularly in the South, local saints see their day celebrated every year as a vehicle for proclaiming municipal identity. In 1987 the city of Bari, for example, celebrated the 900th anniversary of the capture of the relics of Saint Nicholas from Asia Minor. In 1988 the city of Turin commemorated the 100th anniversary of the death of the educator Saint John Bosco. In 1989 the city of Florence celebrated the 600th anniversary of the birth of its patron, the founder of the Abbey of San Marco, Sant'Antonio Pierozzi (1389–1459). An indigenous religion that has thrived for almost two millenia gives saints' anniversaries a populist aura and renders any other civil religion redundant.

A further peculiarity of Italian anniversaries is their local focus. Each city commemorates its native sons, often without regard to an anniversary. In a sense each Italian town has its own civil religion, that of the municipality or what Italians call *campanilismo*. In 1989, for example, the University of Pavia mounted a major conference on Lanfranco di Pavia (c. 1005–1089) to honor a native son who had made his career not in Italy but in Normandy and then as Archbishop of Canterbury. Neither the Normans nor the British paid much attention to a leader who shaped their institutions far more than those of Pavia. In 1988 when Verona mounted an exhibition for the 400th anniversary of the death of the painter Veronese (1528–1588), neighboring Brescia did the same for its painter Moretto (1498–1554), without the pretext of an anniversary. Where cities vie to celebrate favorite sons, the dictates of the Great Calendar matter less. A country in which local loyalties outdo national ones nourishes consensus through annual events more than through anniversaries.

Britain has even less need than Italy to invent a civil religion. In theory the Anglican church performs the function of a civil religion, but because less than 10 percent of the population attends its services, its claim to galvanize the nation lacks conviction. In practice Britain's civil religion centers on the monarchy, which first became the cynosure of national identity under Queen Victoria. By way of exception, victory over Napoleon in 1814 impelled the nation to celebrate the 100th anniversary of George I's accession with a mock naval battle on the Serpentine in London. Indifference disappeared when Queen Victoria's consort Prince Albert brought to Britain from Biedermeier Germany the notion of a prince fulfilling an apolitical role through promoting culture. Prince Albert may be said to have inaugurated the civil religion of the British monarchy.[17] Following his pioneering role in organizing the first universal exposition at the Crystal Palace in 1851, the British royal family has continued to function as sponsors of sport and culture, personifying tradition in the way that German princes did up to 1914. In the civil religion of the British monarchy, anniversaries within the royal family take precedence over any others. The Queen's birthday, the Prince of Wales's wedding anniversary, and the royal jubilees attract more attention than do any historical anniversary. Cultural anniversaries of the sort that constitute civil religion in France, Germany, or Austria run a poor second in Britain.

Continental Europe's cult of anniversaries is in large measure a Biedermeier creation, which competes in Britain with another Biedermeier institution, the civil religion of the royal family. In France, however, the civil religion stems not from Biedermeier attitudes (whose nearest equivalent would be policies of the Restoration of the 1820s) but from the French Revolution. The revolutionary tradition imparts urgency to French anniversaries as each successive regime strives to personify national identity. Because France has changed regimes so often, each new one must reappropriate the Revolution in order to consolidate its place in the civil religion. The bicentennial of the French Revolution, commemorated during 1989 in a crossfire between Mitterand's Socialists and Chirac's Conservatives, was planned in homage to France's civil religion. Since the French public showed much less enthusiasm for all this than had been expected, it remains to be seen whether the boredom manifested in 1989 marks a permanent turning away from a civil religion rooted in revolution.

France's use of revolutionary civil religion to articulate national identity contrasts with Germany's and Austria's Biedermeier habits. As we shall see in Chapter 5, there are two major models for commemorating anniversaries: the French and the German. A commemoration can stress either political ramifications as the French do or apolitical creativity as the Germans do. This dichotomy helps to explain why in Britain Continental styles of commemoration fall flat, except among tourists. Neither the French nor the German model suits a country whose borders are the sea and whose traditions of culture (albeit not of etiquette) prefer eccentricity to conformity. For a British government to invoke political anniversaries like the 400th of the Spanish Armada or the 300th of the Glorious Revolution rings hollow because such events do not underpin national identity the way they would in France or Austria. In Britain the cult of anniversaries is not a native growth but an alien import.

It is in countries where national identity rests on a recently created civil religion, either of politics as in France or of culture as in Germany and Austria, that the cult of anniversaries flourishes. Italy's civil religion, whether of Catholicism or of municipal loyalties, boasts roots too deep to require anniversaries. American civil religion, by way of contrast, stresses neither politics nor religion, but rather symbols that lend themselves better tò annual than to periodic anniversaries. France, Germany, and Austria remain the countries where civil religion reinforces anniversaries.

Anniversaries of Founding Events in the United States

The United States has fashioned a different version of the cult of anniversaries: Americans commemorate events rather than creators. This is because the civil religion of the United States has stressed relatively few themes that promise to bind together people who settled the New World. At the inception of the United States in the 1780s and 1790s, the civil religion of the new republic did not so much supplant the native Protestantism as delimit it.[18] All denominations enjoyed toleration on the condition that none interfere with a civil religion that preached tolerance, veneration for the Founding Fathers and for the Constitution, and respect for certain symbols like the Liberty Bell, the eagle, and the flag. Observances of holidays often echoed gatherings in Protestant meeting houses, as the trappings but not the doctrine of

Protestantism passed into the civil religion. Until well into the twentieth century, public orators in the United States resembled preachers, ceremonial music sounded like that of church hymns, and public gatherings abounded in prayers. Since the end of the Civil War, Americans have preferred annual anniversaries like July 4, Thanksgiving, and Washington's Birthday to periodic ones connected with individuals.

American civil religion, in contrast to the French or the German, actively discourages anniversaries of writers, artists, or musicians. Not even composers as patriotic as Stephen Foster, John Philip Sousa, or George Gershwin belong to America's civil religion. Instead, the practice of toleration invites each ethnic group to commemorate its own luminaries, but forbids any to be imposed upon the nation at large. Consequently, Americans do not add fresh figures to their pantheon of image-carriers the way the French since 1945 have added a writer like Marcel Proust or an artist like Henri Matisse. One reason why Henry Adams got ignored in 1988 is that no intellectual has been inducted into America's civil religion since Thomas Jefferson. American civil religion eschews any deference to creativity.[19]

From the 1780s on, American civil religion faced the task of inculcating a new nationality. This was a more formidable challenge than that of wooing allegiance to a new regime as France or Italy have had to do. Because immigrants included people of every race, religion, and country, American civil religion had to offer an easily understood mythology about America's values. As an additional obstacle, many settlers lived until the 1880s on a frontier where the nation-state scarcely penetrated. Across barriers of distance and disparity, national identity had to rest on plain principles like religious toleration, freedom of opportunity, and the sanctity of the Constitution.

The traumatic event of the Civil War intensified a need for holidays and anniversaries that bind regions of the nation together.[20] The celebration in 1876 of the first centennial of the Declaration of Independence addressed a need to heal regional divisions ten years after the Civil War.[21] Then and now, the United States favored large-scale anniversaries to match the enormous size of the country. American national anniversaries need to be massive, unambiguous, and broad in appeal. To commemorate events dear to one region or interest group would deepen interregional wounds and weaken a sense of class solidarity.

Another new country of British origin, Australia, parallels the United States in emphasizing anniversaries of founding events. The Australian Bicentennial of 1988 celebrated a clear-cut event, the landing of the First Fleet at Sydney Harbor on January 26, 1788, and spent an entire year reinforcing national identity. Like the American bicentennial in 1976, Australia's bicentennial recalled similar commemorations in 1888 and 1938 as well. Emphasis fell on large issues that everyone could grasp like emigration policy, the fate of the Aborigines, and the future of the environment.[22] In contrast to the United States, government funding abounded to assure that the tourist industry would benefit for years to come.

Perhaps the fundamental reason why both Australians and Americans deemphasize cultural luminaries is that in both countries citizens of diverse origin need to be melted into a common nationality. To do so requires commemorating events that people of every ethnic origin share. In the United States events like the first voyage of Columbus, the Declaration of Independence, the Constitutional Convention, and the Civil War transcend ethnic, regional, and religious differences. If Americans were to commemorate native-born cultural figures like Henry Adams, Ralph Waldo Emerson, or H.W. Mencken, such intellectuals might exercise a divisive influence. At the very least they would raise the spectre of class divisions based on education or region. Even more self-defeating would be the commemoration in the United States of European luminaries. Among the rare exceptions, Alexis de Tocqueville was commemorated on the centennial of his death in 1959 and on the 150th anniversary of *Democracy in America* in 1985. He remains one of the few European writers who can draw Americans together.

Still, the need to instill national identity in diverse ethnic groups does not entirely explain why former American luminaries like Benjamin Franklin and Thomas Jefferson have lost their appeal. Franklin's 200th in 1990 passed almost unnoticed. Indeed, he was commemorated more ardently in France than in most regions of the United States. Again, several reasons can be adduced. First, Franklin was an intellectual as well as a statesman, and as such offers diminishing appeal in mass culture. Moreover, his two long sojourns in France tended to make him seem un-American. Second, although the United States retains an eighteenth-century Constitution, fewer and fewer Americans identify any longer with values of the eighteenth century.

By championing modernization, the United States has cut itself off from its eighteenth-century roots. Third, Franklin, like most other American luminaries, personifies a particular region. He is a hero not to the United States as a whole so much as to New England and Pennsylvania. However crucial his contribution to founding the United States, his cultural style reflects the Eastern Seaboard. Southerners, Midwesterners, and Californians feel few bonds with the author of *Poor Richard's Almanac*. This is another way of saying that the United States has grown too large to welcome luminaries of genuinely continental appeal. As a consequence, local museums and historical societies rather than national ones must assume the burden of sponsoring cultural anniversaries.[23]

The separation of church and state in the United States supplies still another reason why national and state governments do not promote anniversaries of luminaries. In Europe state funds routinely finance religious activities. This practice derives from the settlement reached by Napoleon in 1801. In the United States, on the other hand, neither private schools nor universities tap government budgets, even a century after such institutions have dropped a religious affiliation. Likewise, theater, the press, book publishing, and musical performance emerged in Europe under the patronage of princes, while in the United States they emerged as private enterprises that enjoy no tax breaks. Cultural creators in the United States found patrons in the marketplace, whereas similar figures in Europe drew support from government. Even after the United States adopted a program of federal funding for the arts and scholarship in the 1960s, anniversaries of cultural luminaries continue to require private initiative. In the United States no government sponsors anniversaries of writers, composers, and artists, whose careers no government sponsored either.

Of necessity, Americans fall back on anniversaries of symbolic events. A cluster of these since 1986 has allowed Americans to pursue the cult of anniversaries. The centennial of the Statue of Liberty in 1986, the 200th of the Constitutional Convention in 1987, and the 500th of Columbus's discovery of the Americas were planned in such a way as to focus patriotic feeling around easily shared themes.[24] At the regional level, during 1989 and 1990 half a dozen western states commemorated the centennial of statehood, while cities across the country commemorated anniversaries of their founding. Manufacturing corporations, local banks, and insurance companies joined the parade of 50th or 100th anniversaries. Americans satisfy the needs of *homo rhythmicus* by commemorating the founding of corporate bodies, and Europeans do this by celebrating creators. In the United States it is anniversaries of founding events that impart cyclic order to the flow of years.

Notes

1. Abel and Yvonne-Delphée Miroglio, eds., *L'Europe et ses populations* (The Hague: Nijhoff, 1978); articles on 250 "peoples," arranged alphabetically.
2. In the United States after 1787, foreign-born never exceeded 16 percent. I am indebted to historian Robert A. Potash for this information.
3. Orest Ranum, "Counter-Identities of Western European Nations in the Early-Modern Period: Definitions and Points of Departure," in Peter Boerner, ed., *Concepts of National Identity: An Interdisciplinary Dialogue* (Baden-Baden: Nomos, 1986), pp. 63–78.
4. Eric Hobsbawm, "Introduction" and "Mass-Producing Traditions: Europe, 1870–1914," in Hobsbawm and Terence Ranger, eds., *The Invention of Tradition* (Cambridge: Cambridge University Press, 1983), pp. 1–14, 263–307.
5. Benedict Anderson, *Imagined Communities: Reflections on the Origin and Spread of Nationalism* (London: Verso, 1983) examines the role that imagining plays in shaping nationalism around the globe.
6. Mihály Szegedy-Maszák, "The Idea of National Character: A Romantic Heritage," in Boerner, ed., *Concepts of National Identity*, pp. 45–62.
7. William M. Johnston, "A Nation without Qualities: Austria and Its Quest for a National Identity," in Boerner, ed., *Concepts of National Identity*, pp. 177–186.
8. An up-to-date appraisal of European television is Wolfgang Kraus, *Neuer Kontinent Fernsehen: Kultur oder Chaos* (Frankfurt-am-Main: Fischer Taschenbuch Verlag, 1989).
9. On the co-opting of intellectuals by the media, see Régis Debray, *Le Pouvoir intellectuel en France* (Paris: Ramsay, 1979), translated as *Teachers, Writers, Celebrities: The Intellectuals of Modern France* (London: Verso, 1981).
10. A useful guide to these complexities is David B. Barrett, ed., *World Christian Encyclopedia* (New York: Oxford University Press, 1982).
11. Brenda Nelms, *The Third Republic and the Centennial of 1789* (New York: Garland, 1989).
12. A book whose articles document this shift is John Cannon et al., eds.,

The Blackwell Dictionary of Historians (Oxford: Blackwell, 1988).

13. Robert Nisbet, "Civil Religion," *The Encyclopedia of Religion,* 3 (1987): 524.

14. Mona Ozouf, "Revolutionary Religion," in Furet and Ozouf, eds., *A Critical Dictionary of the French Revolution* (Cambridge: Harvard University Press, 1989), pp. 560–570. Emmet Kennedy in *A Cultural History of the French Revolution* (New Haven: Yale University Press, 1989), interprets the entire Revolution as aiming to substitute a civil religion of man for Christianity.

15. Rosamonde Sanson, *Les 14 juillet (1789–1975): Fête et consciences nationales* (Paris: Flammarion, 1976).

16. On the cult of commemorations during the Revolution, see Mona Ozouf, *Festivals and the French Revolution* (Cambridge: Harvard University Press, 1988), pp. 166–186.

17. David Cannadine, "The Context, Performance and Meaning of Ritual: The British Monarchy and the 'Invention of Tradition', c. 1820–1977," in Hobsbawm and Ranger, eds., *The Invention of Tradition,* pp. 101–164.

18. Sidney E. Mead, "The 'Nation with the Soul of a Church'," in Russell E. Richey and Donald G. Jones, eds., *American Civil Religion* (New York: Harper and Row, 1974), pp. 45–75.

19. Jane M. Hatch, ed., *The American Book of Days,* 3d ed. (New York: Wilson, 1978), enumerates thousands of American anniversaries, most of which concern events or political leaders rather than cultural luminaries.

20. Robert N. Bellah, "Civil Religion in America," in Richey and Jones, eds., *American Civil Religion,* pp. 30–33.

21. Robert W. Rydell, *All the World's a Fair: Visions of Empire at American International Expositions, 1876–1916* (Chicago: University of Chicago Press, 1984), pp. 9–37.

22. For the interpretation of painting to enhance national identity, see Daniel Thomas, ed., *Creating Australia: 200 Years of Art 1788–1988* (Adelaide: Art Gallery Board of South Australia, 1988).

23. On local museums, see Warren Leon and Roy Rosenzweig, eds., *History Museums in the United States: A Critical Assessment* (Urbana: University of Illinois Press, 1989).

24. An exhibition concerning the Statue of Liberty produced a probing catalog: New York Public Library, *Liberty: The French-American Salute in Art and History* (New York: Harper and Row, 1986).

4

The Commemoration Industry and the Economic Benefits of Anniversaries

The Commemoration Industry

[handwritten margin notes: Advantage of commemorations; Advance planning]

Commemorations offer a variety of advantages. In the practical sphere, they permit programmers to plan years in advance. In the policy sphere, they enable cultural managers to reinforce national identity. In the economic sphere, they stimulate service industries, which cater to consumers of every sort. The commemoration industry links civil servants, publishers, journalists, manufacturers, performing artists, advertisers, and the travel business in a network of mutual benefit. This chapter explores how the economic benefits of commemorations ripple through local and national economies. Economic clout means that in massive undertakings like the bicentennial of the French Revolution in 1989 and the quincentenary of Columbus's discovery of the Americas in 1992 the commemoration industry largely determines what gets done, and more and more shapes contemporary taste.

The commemoration industry operates at three levels: locally, regionally, and nationally. Because services like hotels, newspapers, urban transport, and tourist agencies flourish in cities, often with little or no connection to neighboring regions, leaders of local enterprises feel an incentive to promote local anniversaries. It is above all for commercial reasons that cities commemorate the anniversary of their founding. Local merchants, hotels, and tourist bureaus cooperate to enhance their town's "image." Among the dozens of town anniversaries that Europe and the United States celebrate every year, the centennial in 1989 of the formation of municipal government in Birmingham, England, was typical for stressing commerce. Seven hundred activities ranging from concerts and parades to canal rides and open houses promoted tourism in the West Midlands of England. It was not local historians who demanded celebration of this rather technical anniversary so much as it was local business. Had the 100th anniversary of Birmingham been overlooked, hardly any "Brummies" would have felt slighted in their self-esteem, but bus companies, theater producers, hoteliers, and restaurant operators would have lost profits. The centennial of Birmingham amounted to a massive tourist campaign.

The same observations apply to events like the centennial of the unveiling of the Statue of Liberty in New York City in 1986, the millennium of Dublin in 1988, or the 800th anniversary of the harbor of Hamburg in 1989. These events attracted tens of thousands of tourists, they won coverage in the press, and they stimulated the souvenir industry. In a very real sense, municipal anniversaries serve commerce more than intellect. They represent a form of local boosterism that suits an era when service industries have replaced manufacturing as a major source of income.

National anniversaries blend commerce and idealism more subtly. Only a cynic would suggest that the bicentennial of the French Revolution in 1989 or New Zealand's 150th anniversary in 1990 or the 700th anniversary of the Swiss Federation in 1991 were motivated solely or even primarily by commercial greed. Formative national events get celebrated above all because in an era of global competition national governments need to cultivate a sense of identity among their citizens. But the venues and activities of such commemorations cannot help but be shaped by the ever-expanding commemoration industry. The same kind of entrepreneurs who profit from municipal commemorations swing into high gear for national ones.

The scope and influence of the commemoration industry revealed itself most glaringly during the bicentennial of the French Revolution. Planned over a period of seven years, and enjoying unprecedented budgets from national and local sources, the bicentennial represented the most massive commemoration that anyone had yet witnessed. In order to proclaim other nations' homage, the Pompidou Center in Paris maintained through 1989 a documentation room that contained hundreds of briefing books listing activities scheduled in more than fifty countries. No other commemoration ever celebrated itself so shamelessly. In France nearly every town organized some kind of recognition of the Revolution, and many smaller ones programmed events throughout the year. The total of bicentennial activities in France outside of Paris numbered in the tens of thousands, while those in Paris numbered many thousands, including hundreds of activities held in downtown Paris during the three days from July 13 to 15. Needless to say, the publicity barrage reached unheard-of intensity. Worldwide television coverage during the weekend of July 14 climaxed months of press reportage, media debates, and publicity campaigns.

In response to this frenzy, the French themselves manifested growing boredom, forcing a number of activities to close for lack of interest and prompting the press to dwell for weeks in advance on fears of traffic congestion in Paris during the mid-July week. Commercial saturation seemed all the more incongruous because the French Revolution was supposed to belong to the Left rather than the Right. Yet few intellectuals of the Left succeeded in raising their voices to "celebrate" the Revolution's contribution to shaping liberal politics, as distinct from "commemorating" its role in shaping beaureaucratic Europe. As many journalists noted, to celebrate implies joining in festivity, while to commemorate implies submitting to conformity. Because the voice of the Left got drowned out in a sea of commercial activity, the whole bicentennial, both in France and abroad, exuded a weary air, creating a mood at odds with the electricity that had filled the air in 1789 and even in 1889. Why did the bicentennial of the French Revolution fail to sustain enthusiasm? Why did the Left fail to exploit the opportunity handed to it by this most massive of historical commemorations?

The simplest answer is that the commemoration industry seized control. In the case of national as well as municipal commemorations, the commemoration industry has expanded to the point where its infrastructure outweighs that of any political party, ideology, or leader. The commemoration industry dictated how the bicentennial of the French Revolution would be commemorated, and not even President Mitterand could resist its exigencies. Because massive commemorations exert a momentum of their own, the Left could shape only a handful of bicentennial events.

In France, as well as in Germany, Italy, and Austria, the infrastructure of commemorations lies in the hands of cultural managers who work as civil servants for national ministries of culture, foreign affairs, education, and tourism, as well as for municipal and regional agencies. By authorizing funds for cultural initiatives, these managers can flood the market with television and radio shows, conferences, museum exhibitions, books and magazines, and historical reenactments. Increasingly, of course, not just government agencies but businesses as well exploit anniversaries. The Great Calendar determines themes of advertising campaigns and the timing of publications; hundreds of titles concerning the French Revolution appeared during 1989. In the streets of Chicago the Sara Lee Corporation financed a gala to celebrate the bicentennial of the French Revolution. The bicentennial was big business, not only for government sponsors of culture but for private enterprise as well. It would be an oversimplification to single out the electronic media or the press or the tourist business or government bureaus for having commercialized the bicentennial. Rather, networks of planners cooperating among these agencies acted to promote not ideology or scholarship but commerce and national image. Caught between the Scylla of commercialism and the Charybdis of national identity, the bicentennial of the Revolution lost all fervor, as business and governmental managers contrived to make tens of thousands of events serve bureaucratic ends. The commemoration industry left too little room for spontaneity.

Commercial Overkill during the French Revolutionary Bicentennial

It is worth examining a few examples of how the bicentennial stifled enthusiasm through a combination of commercial overkill and government overstatement. Everyone who visited Paris during the spring and summer of 1989 saw shop windows (particularly in pastry shops and clothing stores) festooned with tricolors, Phrygian bonnets, and miniature Bastilles. Contrary to expectations, however, the motif of the guillotine fizzled as a marketing device. T-shirts and underpants featuring golden brown guillotines disappeared from stores, while Phrygian bonnets and images of Liberty proliferated. During June and July street vendors of memorabilia abounded to the point of nausea. Endless presentation of the same goods sated the most patient strollers within days. Similarly, costume pageants staged at Versailles on May 4 and throughout the summer at the Tuileries Gardens quickly palled.

The privately financed theme park at the Tuileries, which had been planned to attract twenty thousand visitors a day, was lucky to attract one thousand. By June everyone was tired of seeing brown fustian clothes and hearing the *carmagnole*. In short, the bicentennial elicited the indifference that is the reward of saturation advertising. The campaign should have ended after three months; instead it ran for an entire year.

As if the commercialism of the bicentennial was not controversial enough, defenders of the Revolution suffered the further handicap that planners telescoped events from the period of 1789 to 1794 into a single year's commemoration. The Terror of 1793 and 1794 was on the agenda fully as much as events of 1789. This happened because both popular memory and professional historians compress the five years of Revolution into a single narrative. Moreover, the organizers seemed to fear, rightly as it turned out, that interest in the Revolution would wane after a single year, so that everything had to be squeezed into one paroxysm of commemorating.

To a degree that no one could have foreseen in 1982 when the bicentennial was first planned, the packaging of the entire Revolution into one year's activities worked to the detriment of the Left because the interpretation of those years that found widest favor was anti-revolutionary. Throughout the 1980s, more and more historians were interpreting the Revolution in a way that undermined the whole endeavor. Instead of having founded a stable new order, the Revolution was said to have unleashed a prolonged civil war.[1] In best-selling books, François Furet and Simon Schama took the lead in arguing that the violence we associate with the Terror began in 1789.[2] They asserted that from start to finish, the French Revolution favored random killing. What made this view awkward for partisans of the Revolution to rebut was the assumption that the five years had to be handled as a unit. By pervading bicentennial activities, this assumption muffled any discourse from the Left about the benefits of specific events like the Declaration of the Rights of Man and the Citizen or the selling of church land. Although the guillotine fizzled as a marketing device, it haunted historians. Their skepticism tended to make the commercialism seem pointless.

To make matters worse for the Left, a great deal of publicity, both inside and outside France, concerned the region of the Vendée south of Nantes, where local leaders mounted protests (including the production of a feature film) against the Revolution itself as well as against the bicentennial. The Vendéens, whose ancestors had lost perhaps a hundred thousand victims to the Terror, helped to organize what became known as the counterbicentennial, and foreign journalists publicized these protests almost as much as they did the official celebrations.[3] The Counterbicentennial attracted far more publicity than its size warranted, and it too made a mockery of the Phrygian caps and tricolors that filled souvenir stalls.

A less commercial example of how the infrastructure of commemorations dominated the bicentennial was the incorporation of incongruous events into it. Because the National Commission for the Bicentennial decided to emphasize the Declaration of the Rights of Man and the Citizen, the theme of civil rights during any period could get governmental funding. The Ministry of Culture commissioned dozens of works in conjunction with the bicentennial, including an opera that premiered on October 8 in the cathedral of Arras, the birthplace of Robespierre. What would that misguided puritan have thought of a bicentennial opera whose libretto by Eugène Ionesco concerns the twentieth-century Franciscan Maximilian Kolbe, who starved to death in order to save prisoners at Auschwitz? No doubt it was laudable of the French state to sponsor an opera with a libretto by France's most famous dramatist, but what had Auschwitz to do with 1789? It sounded as though the French were claiming to have invented civil rights. Just before July 14, Mrs. Thatcher had the nerve to point out the implausibility of such a claim. No wonder the French and foreigners alike could not discern what the bicentennial was commemorating. Confusion of purpose left many thinking that the year's events had served mainly a commercial function.

Another disadvantage in the mass marketing of commemorations came to light through the observation by parents of how children responded to the bicentennial. Teenagers, who usually like fads, quickly tired of this one because they found the timing arbitrary. If the French Revolution is as important as the media during 1989 said it was, children asked: "Why don't people pay attention to it every year?" Children do not understand why adults allow anniversaries to monopolize the agenda of public discourse. They are too young to need rhythms punctuating the flow of years. "Here today, gone tomorrow" is the motto of the commemoration industry, and its atmosphere of ephemerality undermines serious discussion. Parisians will probably remember the souvenir booths of 1989 longer than the televised debates.

One may well join French children in asking: Why has the infrastructure of commemorations preempted public discourse about the past? In particular, why does commercial indulgence pervade commemorations of national, and not just local, events? As we have seen, the postmodern age suffers a lack of consensus as to what merits attention. Anniversaries fill a vacuum left by the absence of any deeper consensus; cultural managers agree about little else except the utility of anniversaries in programming events. But because European countries commemorate so many anniversaries every year, each celebration tends to ignore the others, intensifying competition and making each an end in itself. Without anyone noticing, a capitalist free market in commemorations has displaced socialist planning of them. Although the Revolutionary bicentennial provided an umbrella organization for coordinating local events, the result was duplication of parades, re-enactments, and exhibitions nationwide. An unregulated market in commemorations represents a triumph of the capitalist Right over the socialist Left, and one result was the directionless extravaganza that France mounted during 1989.

A second factor encourages the ubiquity of the commemoration industry. Anniversaries exist not so much to honor the past as to help cultural managers award subsidies. Since cultural budgets have to be spent, anniversaries provide a hassle-free way of scheduling controversial events without offending voters. The abundance of commemorations confirms Europe's withdrawal from ideologies. Viewed in this light, the bicentennial of the French Revolution never offered the Left a chance to parade its ideas. Rather, from the beginning the bicentennial favored the agendas of commercial and governmental bureaucracies, which thrive on contriving pseudoconsensus. The mobilizing of national self-image to enhance profits also benefits the Right more than the Left.

The bicentennial of the French Revolution was the biggest historical commemoration ever undertaken. Its organizers spent more money, embraced more countries and cities, and mounted more events than ever before. P.T. Barnum's ethos of "Bigger and better" came to life with a French twist. Yet failure to excite the public could have been and was predicted, for gigantic commemorations exist not so much to arouse enthusiasm as to justify stewardship of culture by government and business. In eliciting cultural patronage, as well as in promoting tourism, the bicentennial proved singularly successful, even if it failed to stimulate political discourse. Since major anniversaries serve government and business sponsors more directly than they do the public, organizers who wish to evade the maw of the commemoration industry would do well to embrace unfamiliar topics.

The Business of Commemorations in the United States

Americans excel at commemorating not individual creators but rather events from their national and local history. Unfolding on the national, state, and town level, historical anniversaries in the United States combine commercial exploitation with proclaiming national and local identity. By a peculiar irony, many American commemorations emphasize commercialism less than do massive European ones like the Revolutionary bicentennial. The American Civil War, for example, underwent four years of reenactments during its centennial between 1961 and 1965. Fifteen years later the American Revolutionary War Reenactment Society mounted "living history" on the 200th anniversary of major battles. Even more popular is the series of Civil War reenactments that took place during the 125th anniversary from 1986 to 1990. In July 1988, for example, the Battle of Gettysburg was reenacted by thousands of uniformed participants, most of whom came to Gettysburg to have fun rather than to further a commercial extravaganza. In 1990 more effectively than in 1965, Civil War commemorations solidify regional loyalties while promoting a modicum of tourism and abetting the unceasing flow of books on America's great trauma. In view of the importance of America's civil religion in bonding disparate regions together, reenactments of the Civil War may be said to belong to the rituals of the civil religion.

As in Europe, municipal anniversaries in the United States emphasize economic boosterism, but often with more idealism than in Europe. In 1989 the city of Troy, New York, for example, celebrated the 200th anniversary of its founding. Even though the bulk of the activities concentrated on wooing tourists and strengthening economic infrastructure, Troy proudly claimed to have enhanced America's self-image by inspiring the symbol of "Uncle Sam," who, according to local legend, was a Troy manufacturer around 1812 named Samuel Wilson. In a nation as vast as the United States, where citizens easily feel overwhelmed by the sheer size of government, it benefits everyone for a city to celebrate its uniqueness. However much local businesses profit from commemorations, Americans have not fostered a commemoration industry to compare with what France generated during 1989. A certain idealism persists in American regional celebrations, perhaps because governmental planning bulks so much smaller than in Europe.

In recent years a notably cheerful atmosphere has attended the commemoration of statehood, particularly in the Northwest. During 1989 the states of North Dakota, South Dakota, Montana, and Washington celebrated 100th anniversaries, followed in 1990 by Wyoming and Idaho. These six states promoted their self-image in a relatively disinterested way. Reenactments, publications, and tourist events unfolded in a spirit of cooperation among the six. Outdoor parties at the state capitols and promotion of tourist attractions like Mount Rushmore in South Dakota and Yellowstone National Park in Wyoming proliferated. To be sure, the commemoration industry required that collectibles like guns, knives, flags, belts, and bumper stickers would abound. On April 22, 1989, the state of Oklahoma reenacted the Land Rush of 1889, when the Indian Territory was thrown open to land claims. Although inevitably this commemoration elicited anniversary tomahawks, it also inspired discussion of Indian land rights.

In 1992 the United States, together with countries of the Hispanic world, will commemorate the 500th anniversary of Columbus's discovery of the Americas. This is the kind of shaping event that American commemorators relish. Unlike the American bicentennial of 1976 or the bicentennial of the Constitution in 1987, the quincentenary of Columbus's voyage involves coordination with many other countries. All the Latin American nations feel equally if not more committed to celebrating a Spanish-speaking explorer, who landed in the Caribbean. Seizing the lead, Spain is holding the Olympic Summer Games in Barcelona as well as mounting a world's fair in Seville. The latter will be only the fourth top-grade universal exposition held since 1940; the others were in Brussels in 1958, Montreal in 1967, and Osaka in 1970.

In all the Hispanic countries, the commemoration industry has swung into action, investing in infrastructure, planning commercial exploitation, and launching vast publicity campaigns. Spain has grasped the quincentenary as an incentive to construct a high-speed railroad between Madrid and Seville, as well as to renovate the telephone system in Madrid, Seville, and Barcelona. Urged on by Israel, Spain has also shouldered the challenge of commemorating the achievements of medieval Jewish culture on the occasion of the 500th anniversary of the expulsion of the Jews. In Italy Columbus's hometown of Genoa launched in 1987 a five-year plan of upgrading its tourist facilities. The United States has made a less flashy commitment to refurbishing all sites in the National Park System where Hispanics settled, particularly in Florida, Texas, and California. Last but not least, replicas of Columbus's three vessels are being built in Japan to reenact the voyage.

The Columbus quincentenary motivates commercial activity through local self-promotion beneath an overlay of idealism. The voyage fits the theme of global interdependence that will overshadow the decade of the nineties. Genoa, Seville, Barcelona, Miami, Caracas, San Antonio, and San Diego among many others will share in commemorating a Hispanic initiative. The fact that business investment will dominate the commemoration may be seen by some as reenforcing a North American mode of hegemony over the continents that Columbus brought into the European orbit. Whatever critics may say, commercial investment represents a principal mode of late twentieth-century celebration. To improve a region's transportation and hotels allows commemorations to leave lasting benefits.

As a final irony, to commemorate the European "discovery" of the Americas opens painful questions about colonial mistreatment of indigenous peoples. It is doubtful whether any North or South American Indians will wish to "celebrate" Columbus. Nevertheless, the quincentenary will offer a platform for Amerindians to reflect how commercialism has denatured their inheritance. No amount of American federal investment in Hispanic sites or in Indian reservations can compensate for the uprooting of Indian civilization. The outpouring of investment in Spain and North America provides an incentive for critics to propose a more modest, Indian-centered reflection on Columbus's arrival. The propensity of the commemoration industry to invest in tourist facilities can be corrected through Indian initiatives to promote conservation.

Both in Europe and the United States, because of ease in scheduling and in commanding consensus, anniversaries promote tourism fully as much as they enhance national identity. Commemorations resemble the Olympic Games in nourishing the service industries that underpin postindustrial societies. By tapping the civil religion of republics, anniversaries mobilize consensus to commit resources more lavishly than any other peacetime activity can match. As leisure hours increase, every country will invest more and more in attractions that excite its own citizens and woo foreigners. Commemorations provide the most convenient and least controversial device to coordinate such identity-building endeavors. Throughout the 1990s as military budgets shrink, commemoration budgets will grow.

Notes

1. D.M.G. Sutherland, *France 1789–1815: Revolution and Counterrevolution* (New York: Oxford University Press, 1986), and Jacques Solé, *Questions of the French Revolution: A Historical Overview* (New York: Pantheon, 1989).
2. François Furet and Mona Ozouf, eds., *A Critical Dictionary of the French Revolution* (Cambridge, Mass: Harvard University Press, 1989) and Simon Schama, *Citizens: A Chronicle of the French Revolution* (New York: Knopf, 1989).
3. Reynald Secher, *Le génocide franco-français: La Vendée vengée* (Paris: Presses Universitaires de france, 1986), which disclosed previously unsuspected casualty figures from the Vendée, got wide newspaper coverage. French intellectuals debated these issues in Pierre Nora, ed., " '89 La Commémoration," *Le Débat*, Nr. 57 (November-December 1989), 1–224.

5

Courtly Traditions and National Styles of Commemoration

The Cult of Anniversaries as a Legacy of Courtly Practices

The cult of anniversaries reflects the conditions of the nineteenth century in which it arose. As we have noted, two different traditions of government lie behind the emergence of anniversaries. On the one hand, leaders of the French Revolution adopted anniversaries as a way to consolidate national identity. On the other hand, courtiers in German principalities of the eighteenth and early nineteenth centuries pioneered many practices that live on in the cult of anniversaries. The civil service tradition of the French interacts with the courtier tradition of the Germans to shape European attitudes toward commemorations. This chapter will look at ways in which the bourgeois takeover of courtly models has interlocked with civil service traditions to foster today's cult of anniversaries. The prestige of the courtly tradition in Europe illuminates, moreover, why Americans have not adopted cultural anniversaries of luminaries with the same alacrity as have Europeans.

Since the 1970s conferences, symposia, and academic meetings have proliferated, with or without anniversaries to justify them. This is partly because the volume of scholarly publications has swollen out of control. Because even the most industrious scholars can no longer survey works pertinent to their field, everyone must rely on contacts established at formal and informal gatherings. The popularity of networking among professionals has arisen in response to an overload of stimuli. Conferences help scholars and intellectuals to keep track of developments, while anniversaries supply the themes. By focusing the topic of conferences, particularly in the humanities, the cult of anniversaries helps to channel an oversupply of publications. Amid a plethora of possible conferences, the Great Calendar suffices to justify as many as possible.

A protypical commemoration in Europe involves a conference or an exhibition held in a former castle, palace, or monastery. The speakers spend two or three days as guests in a princely environment, being wined and dined beneath frescoed ceilings and amid baroque vistas. Whether the premises belong to the state, the church, or an aristocratic family, simply being there boosts everyone's self-esteem. The guests feel honored, as though a prince had summoned them to share his palace for a weekend. Local and sometimes national dignitaries grace the occasion, while theater performances and tourist excursions enhance the conviviality. The organizers of such extravaganzas function like servants of a princely court, providing royal hospitality devoid of urban hassles.

In the United States commemorative conferences take place in the faculty center of a university, or in a hotel, and the organizers are faculty colleagues who bestow scant sense of largesse. American conferences tend to resemble a three-day cruise on an ocean liner, where the setting reminds one of the present, while in Europe they resemble a sojourn at a princely court, where customs from the past abound. The amenities of an American campus or hotel staffed by fellow academics cannot match those of the Hofburg in Vienna, the Palace of the Popes in Avignon, or the Castel dell'Ovo in Naples staffed by professional courtiers. There conferences unfold amid frescoes, rococo gardens, or romanesque cloisters and may include excursions to sites associated with the anniversary. American universities cannot hope to compete in panache or antiquity.

However ingeniously commemorators use Europe's palaces, monasteries, and stately homes, the courtly analogy extends beyond mere physical setting and style of hospitality. A whole ethos is involved. The courtly model of anniversaries derives from German courts in the eighteenth century. The classic example of a small principality that elevated writers into courtiers was that of Weimar in Thuringia, until recently part of the German Democratic Republic. Between the 1770s and the 1820s Weimar's prince Karl August (ruled 1775–1828) attracted to his court not only the titan Johann Wolfgang von Goethe

(1749–1832) and his friend Friedrich Schiller (1759–1805), but the historian and court preacher Johann Gottfried Herder (1744–1803) and the writer Christoph Martin Wieland (1733–1813) as well. Later, Franz Liszt and the addled Friedrich Nietzsche would settle there too. A princely territory of just a few hundred square kilometers, Weimar encompassed a court theater, public works, and a small bureaucracy, all of which offered a microcosm of German ideals. The Weimar court was at once diminutive in scale, intelligent in policy, and vaulting in ambition. Its combination of Faustian scope and Lilliputian scale lives on in many commemorations.

German and Austrian commemorations often aspire to recreate "Weimar for a day" by bringing luminaries to a country setting and asking them to thresh out world-shaking questions on a tiny stage. Cosmic issues get aired within an august setting as though the conference were recreating a neoclassical court like that of Goethe's Weimar. Just as Goethe wrote *Faust* in the same idyllic setting where Schiller composed heaven-storming dramas like *Wallenstein*, so today's intellectuals get invited to canvass the world's problems in a pastoral paradise like Schloss Leopoldskron outside Salzburg or the Villa Serbelloni on Lake Como. German — and even more, Austrian — etiquette still emphasizes titles, precedence, and portentousness just as it did in Goethe's day, so that solemnity hovers in rarefied air.

After 1815 the German courts developed what is known as the Biedermeier style, which may be described as a middle-class version of the princely ethos. Throughout southern Germany and Austria the middle classes emulated the values and life-style of the eighteenth-century aristocracy. Civil servants were recruited from the middle classes, who prized the same ideals of peace, productivity, and local authority as had their aristocratic predecessors. The Biedermeier ethos tamed for the middle classes Goethe's Olympian titanism, as the giant of Weimar became a model for middle-class consumers of culture.

Biedermeier veneration of titans lives on in many cultural occasions today. Any commemoration of a cultural giant evokes the sense of disproportion that prevailed at the court of Weimar between the genius of Goethe and Schiller and the triteness of their fellow townspeople.[1] Inevitably, the gap between genius and ordinary folks comes to the fore at any conference that celebrates genius. The court at Weimar institutionalized this gap by creating an etiquette to deal with it. Courtly etiquette allowed poets to function in the community without becoming the intimidating poseurs that the French call "sacred monsters." The Weimar court integrated its geniuses into the community without overawing the townspeople or inflating the geniuses. Such fruitful encounter between genius and people is what any commemoration envisions, inviting today's bourgeoisie to sup at the table of yesterday's titans.

Etiquette such as the Weimar court perfected provides a framework that helps commemorators to confront great shapers of culture. It is easier to interpret a titan if one is frequenting a palace or castle such as that figure might have visited. The setting heightens respect for the celebrand. Although some Americans may disdain such rituals, they have the virtue of making genius accessible. To discuss great literature or art in a palace attended by courtiers humanizes a celebrand without debasing his genius, since the setting suggests that the creator once enjoyed a distinguished place in his community. The courtly tradition of lionizing genius has a further advantage. It challenges the myth of artistic Bohemia, which holds that the ablest creators must repudiate bourgeois society in order to flourish.[2] The cult of the avant-garde, which arose in Paris after 1830, found no place at the German courts, which as late as the 1880s kept geniuses like Wagner and Liszt as darlings of society. In France after 1880 the mores of the avant-garde drove painters like Gauguin and Van Gogh to the fringes of society, while German courts like that of Munich kept painters such as Lenbach and Boecklin in the public eye.

The German model suits anniversary commemorations, whose purpose after all is to bring creators into the mainstream. Conferences and exhibitions that rehabilitate rebels like Baudelaire, Rimbaud, Verlaine, and Gauguin interpret them in the light of a pattern of life they despised. Postmoderns have abandoned the myth of the isolated artist battling against an uncomprehending society. We want to see even the most quirky figures silhouetted against bourgeois life. The German courtly model (which the Emperor Napoleon III brought to France during the 1850s a few years after Prince Albert had brought it to Britain) offers a painless way to do so. Commemorations in a princely setting have the effect of subjecting to bourgeois scrutiny artists who may have devoted their careers to evading it. Figures who were rebels, isolates, or debauchees now get their day as posthumous guests of royalty.

Anniversaries came to the fore during the transition from aristocratic to bourgeois hegemony between 1815 and 1870. They offered a way for the newly ascendant middle classes to appropriate the legacy of the aristocracy. By sponsoring anniversary commemorations of giants like Luther, Raphael, Rubens, Leibniz, and Goethe, all of whom had flourished in princely courts, the middle classes were claiming these clients of the aristocracy as their own. After 1815 and even more conspicuously after 1850, anniversaries provided a way for the bourgeoisie to place a stamp of approval on artists and writers who had blossomed under courtly patronage. During the late nineteenth century the cult of anniversaries ratified a changing of the guard in Europe's cultural establishment.

What sociologists call a shift in cultural hegemony took place when a new class began to sponsor cultural activities.[3] Not only did anniversaries help the middle classes to sort out preferences among artists of the courtly epoch, but they provided a teaching device as well. Aristocracies that had followed a traditional calendar of family occasions and church feasts had no need for a national calendar of luminaries. But the bourgeoisie who entered upon this heritage relatively untutored needed a grid of anniversaries to clarify cultural loyalties that had originated outside their tradition. Anniversaries constitute a teaching device to help newcomers orient themselves among cultural treasures. Commemorations still serve this purpose. At about the same time that public picture galleries were replacing princes' cabinets of curiosities and vernacular encyclopedias and journals were disseminating scholarship, calendars of secular anniversaries were replacing family and church lore as a device for marshalling homage.

Several French projects of the 1840s illustrate the bourgeois appetite for cultural reorientation. In 1849 the French sociologist Auguste Comte published his "Positivist Calendar," which assigned a luminary to every day of the year and named months for Dante, Gutenberg, Shakespeare, Descartes, and Frederick the Great.[4] In 1848 the visionary painter Paul-Joseph Chenavard received a commission from the French Second Republic to paint murals in the Pantheon of Paris depicting the major stages of Europe's cultural ascent. If the project had not been aborted, it would have portrayed hundreds of luminaries who to this day constitute the staple of European anniversaries.[5] Another French painter who succeeded (where Chenavard failed) in persuading the middle classes to identify with their predecessors was Pierre Puvis de Chavannes (1824–1898), who from the 1870s through the 1890s decorated Republican universities, museums, and town halls with generalized antique figures to symbolize Europe's heritage. For similar reasons Bostonians hired him in the 1890s to decorate the grand staircase of their new library. Puvis's innocuously antique figures helped the new middle classes to identify with ancient Greece and Rome.[6] They reinforced the message of classroom and Republican rostrum that France was the eldest daughter not so much of the church as of classical antiquity and that France spoke for humanity as a whole. Anniversaries in France still deliver that message.

In Vienna similar goals accompanied the historicizing epoch that ran from the 1860s to the 1890s. Wall paintings on buildings of the Ringstrasse such as the Burgtheater, the Parliament, and the Kunsthistorisches Museum invited the bourgeoisie to identify with ancient Greece and Rome. In 1879 the painter Hans Makart organized a celebration of Emperor Franz Joseph's twenty-fifth wedding anniversary by staging a procession modeled on imagery from Rubens's Antwerp. Display of affinity with the baroque painter and his Catholic city provided another way for middle classes to appropriate courtly culture.

Courtly style still prevails at German, Austrian, Italian, and French anniversary commemorations. In hundreds of European cities, bourgeois intellectuals now discourse where nobles once dallied. An American variant is the pseudocourtly style imparted to luxury hotels in the later nineteenth or early twentieth centuries. Hotels are America's palaces. Up to the 1920s luxury hotels imitated the interiors of palaces, while during the 1920s art deco evolved as an industrial variant that substituted mass-produced metalwork for the art nouveau that had prevailed around 1900. In the United States art deco interiors are still favored for grand hotels, movie theaters, skyscrapers, ocean liners, and palaces of the nouveaux riches. Gatherings in a plush hotel represent an American way of paying homage to European forebears, whose achievements may have been aped but not equaled. In Europe comparable events unfold in palaces, monasteries, or castles, whose settings allow the bourgeoisie to preen in the halls of the class they ousted.

Anniversary occasions that convene in museums, palaces, and abbeys recall the transition whereby the middle classes seized hegemony. In a sense all European anniversaries that honor events or figures from before 1789 celebrate this changing of the guard. Through the cult of anniversaries, today's middle class and working class tighten their grip on a heritage that their forebears expropriated during the nineteenth century. Anniversary commemorations remain at bottom celebrations of a cultural coup d'etat whose victors seek to legitimate their hegemony. The cult of anniversaries has become a ritual of civil religion, which acknowledges that what had seemed "natural" to the aristocracy represents an acquisition to the bourgeoisie. By helping the middle classes to assimilate what they had expropriated, anniversaries from before 1789 help the bourgeoisie to feel at home in a world they inherited but did not make.

The situation is more ambiguous in Britain. One reason why the British do not emphasize cultural anniversaries as ardently as the Germans or the French is that Britain outgrew its Old Regime rather than overthrew it. Through parliamentary reform between the 1830s and the 1880s, the political system evolved to incorporate the middle classes and then the working classes in the House of Commons, while permitting the landed families to retain their status. After a period of imposing confiscatory taxation between 1918 and the 1970s, the middle classes have come during the past decade to esteem the estates of the aristocracy as national treasures.[7] Moreover, no one in Britain stands to gain by recalling, as Henry James liked to do in novels like *The Portrait of a Lady* (1881), the ascent of middle-class heiresses into the aristocracy, and this concealment of upward assimilation further undermines any call for anniversaries. No cult of anniversaries is needed where the transfer of hegemony took place so quietly. Anniversaries appeal to new owners, not ancestral ones.

The cult of anniversaries thrives in countries like France, Germany, Austria, and Italy, which have undergone frequent changes of regime. Today's political class there declares itself the heirs of yesterday's by commemorating their predecessors' anniversaries. The more often regimes have changed, the more irresistible the impulse to contrast today's stability to yesterday's upheavals. Thus Germany and Austria endeavor to counter the trauma of the Hitler years by commemorating earlier phases of their past. In 1983 Austria endeavored to make people realize what a risk Europe had run three hundred years before when the Turks came within a day or two of starving Vienna into submission. The fate of the United States never hung by such a slender thread as that, and Americans know it.

In 1989, through the most lavish of commemorations, the French

Fifth Republic aspired to legitimate its role as the successor of the first four republics and of the monarchies that preceded it. There having been at least fifteen regimes in France since 1789, this bewildering array makes commemorations an ideal way to sort out which ones still carry significance. There is, moreover, ample precedent for courting legitimacy through celebrations. Napoleon III courted approval when in 1855 he strove to surpass the London Universal Exhibition of four years earlier. He did so again during the Universal Exposition of 1867.[8] Likewise, the innumerable events in celebration of the French Revolutionary bicentennial in 1989 affirm the Fifth Republic's claim to have incorporated what was best in the fifteen regimes that preceded it since 1789.

How different is the United States, which has enjoyed a single regime (i.e., constitution) since 1787. Because major institutions have enjoyed such a high degree of continuity, Americans feel less need to relive the ups and downs of their past. In the United States, moreover, the middle classes did not seize control from an older class, as they did in Europe. Except in parts of the South, it was the middle classes that founded the society. Consequently, the United States underwent no transfer of hegemony as dramatic as that which occurred in Europe since 1789. The thesis that the cult of anniversaries celebrates the triumph of the bourgeoisie helps to explain why the United States has minimized that cult's emphasis on creators. Anniversaries of luminaries bridge gaps between heterogeneous regimes and weave threads of continuity across gulfs of understanding. Heirs of stability scarcely need to commemorate their good fortune by exalting artists and writers.

If anniversaries help a nation to assimilate a tumultuous past, the same incentive seldom exists for corporate bodies. Universities, museums, academies, industrial corporations, and clubs prefer to ignore previous crises, something which nations find it harder to accomplish. Whereas nation-states invoke anniversaries in order to digest upheavals, private bodies choose to conceal vicissitudes rather than commemorate them. This suggests still another reason why the United States does not emphasize anniversaries. Apart from the Civil War, which has been commemorated as ardently as any event in Europe, the American nation has weathered no cataclysms, and American private bodies see little reason to hail a record of continuity. One reason that the centennial of the Statue of Liberty in 1986, the bicentennial of the American Constitution in 1987, and the bicentennial of the First Presidential Inauguration in 1989 never sparked popular debate was that these occasions evoked no memories of crisis. They marked instead a national continuity, which most Americans feel never wavered. The United States has not experienced a series of upheavals the way modern France, Germany, Austria, and Italy have. Except in the case of the Civil War, American history has flowed too smoothly to require anniversaries. Still less do Americans have a courtly past that they can deploy during commemorations. There are no abbeys in which to convene conferences and no palaces in which to perform theater. Mansions of the wealthy are a poor substitute for castles.[9] Neither the German model of princely courts nor the French model of revolutionary triumphs suits American level-headedness.

Crises needed for anniversaries

French and German Prototypes

The contrast between French and German styles of commemoration goes beyond the difference between courtiers and revolutionaries. Age-old differences between French and German modes of nationhood get reflected in modes of commemoration. Already in 1789 the national identity of the French was self-congratulatory, for the country had attained "natural" frontiers a hundred years before, its capital city had functioned as such for nearly eight hundred years, and the revolutionary state needed only to assert its role as administrator of a wealthy and far-flung nation. Inevitably, rituals of identity, which anticlericals introduced during the 1790s derived from those of their adversary, the Catholic church. To cite a graphic example, the Jacobins in 1793 converted the hilltop church of Paris's patron Sainte Geneviève into a Pantheon of worthies. It received the bodies of Republican saints like Voltaire and Rousseau, whose remains were exhumed and transferred to the hallowed spot. Pilgrimages to Paris were encouraged, outdoor festivals echoed Catholic worship, and a new calendar replaced saints' days with those of Enlightenment luminaries. All of these devices, including anniversaries of events from just a year or two before, reinforced a thriving sense of national identity.

The situation was very different in Germany, where as late as the 1850s nationhood represented a distant aspiration. No nation-state existed, no natural frontiers cried out to be ratified, and no single church, either Protestant or Catholic, united the population. During the first half of the nineteenth century, partisans of German nation-hood had no institutions on which to build. In their place intellectuals glorified past achievements as a means of mobilizing potential. Amidst yearning for nationhood, intellectuals made anniversaries a pretext for proclaiming German greatness. The students who in 1817 celebrated the 300th anniversary of Luther's posting of the Ninety-five Theses by marching to the Wartburg and igniting bonfires near the spot where he had translated the Bible were inventing a new mode of propa-ganda. The grandest example of a literary anniversary carrying politi-cal impact came when towns all over Germany honored the poet Friedrich Schiller on the centennial of his birth in 1859. The Schiller-fests fanned impatience for German unification, and the mood of urgency carried over into the 1860s.[10] The 50th anniversary of the Battle of the Nations at Leipzig, celebrated in 1863, performed a similar function.

By a peculiar irony, 1990, the year of German reunification, marked the 800th anniversary of the death of a medieval emperor, Frederick Barbarossa (c. 1125–1190), whom legend links with just such a turn-ing point. Saga relates that the emperor will sleep atop the Kyffhäuser peak west of Halle in East Germany until such time as the German realm reunites. What better way to celebrate the reunification of Ger-many in 1990 than to stage a rally atop the Kyffhäuser on June 10, 1990, the 800th anniversary of Frederick's death? Such an occasion would have commemorated the German origins of the cult of anniver-saries.

Other peoples who aspired to form a nation-state exploited cultural anniversaries in similar fashion. In 1865 the Czechs commemorated the 450th anniversary of the martyrdom of Jan Hus. In the same year the newly unified Italians commemorated the 600th anniversary of the birth of Dante, followed by the 500th anniversary of the death of Petrarch in 1878. Secular intellectuals identified with literary giants who had forged the Italian language and proclaimed national poten-tial. Cultural patriarchs won such intense devotion that celebrations of their anniversaries set the tone for civil ceremonies. Mussolini's Fas-cists commemorated the most improbable figures, including proto-Fascist martyrs like the lad Balilla who had resisted the Austrians in 1746. Peoples who aspired to nationhood or had only recently achieved it cultivated anniversaries with an intensity that proved contagious.

The present-day cult of anniversaries has fused the twin sources of

French Revolutionary rituals and German cultural anniversaries into something more widespread than either. Differences between German and French conceptions cut deep. The Germans brought a Protestant sense of vocation to the task of exalting predecessors. They honor geniuses like Dürer, Leibniz, Kant, and Beethoven for having towered above the nation, while the French like their luminaries to blend into it as into the Catholic communion of saints. German prophets stand out from one another the way Luther, Schiller, and Wagner did, while French men of letters merge into a single current the way Montaigne, Molière, and Montesquieu do. The French like to revere the stream as a whole, while the Germans extol spectacular individuals for having transcended it. The French value exemplars who affirm existing traits, while the Germans esteem those who devised new ways to be German. The French expect their luminaries to confirm what it already means to be French, while the Germans expect their geniuses to transform what it means to be German.

As a result German anniversaries tend to celebrate geniuses like Grünewald, Goethe, and Nietzsche, while French anniversaries tend to honor carriers of time-honored qualities like Montaigne, Rameau, and Poussin. Germans commemorate creative genius, while the French honor finesse. Today's cult of anniversaries cannot help mirroring these two poles: some celebrands like Montesquieu personify national or regional traits, while others like Rousseau outsoar the confines of tradition to pioneer new attitudes. By a peculiar paradox, the French tend to stress traditional values to an extent that is almost courtly, while the Germans emphasize innovation with a zeal that is almost revolutionary. The French boast that their tradition thrives, while the Germans dream of fostering innovation. The French want to reinvigorate Montaigne and Racine, while the Germans want to unleash new Schillers and new Hegels. In a supreme reversal of roles, the French exploit rituals that derive from the Great Revolution in order to proclaim devotion to tradition, while the Germans deploy a courtly panoply in order to praise innovation.

These French and German prototypes shed light on why Americans fancy cultural anniversaries less than do Europeans. Americans have never based their national identity on intellectual prowess, not even on that of figures as versatile, or if you will as European, as Benjamin Franklin or Thomas Jefferson. The United States had produced hardly any intellectual giants to invoke from a prenational past, nor did it subsequently groom exemplars of good taste and consummate workmanship the way the French did. Rather the United States unfolded in a process of westward expansion whose heroes remained local or anonymous. Continental sweep, the primacy of commerce, and the separation of church and state precluded America's developing a pantheon of cultural heroes. The country expanded too far too fast for regional notables to reap national prestige. No folk heroes like Davy Crockett, or composers like Stephen Foster, or writers like Mark Twain could claim the status of national icons that fell to Luther and Goethe, or Rabelais and Racine. Until recently Europe's luminaries thrived in what remained a courtly culture, while America's found no such haven to adorn. If the cult of anniversaries derives from the courts of the eighteenth century, it was against these very courts that the American colonies rebelled. Americans forged an anticourtly culture that continues to shun those epitomes of courtly grace, cultural anniversaries.

However readily post-1945 Europe has adopted democracy, it has retained a courtly apparatus of patronage. The agencies that sponsor commemorations derive from bourgeois adaptation of aristocratic ways. After the Renaissance, princes founded universities as well as academies of science and the arts in order to enlist creativity to serve the state. In Europe princes founded nearly all the museums and libraries, and in the case of Italy it was a conquering prince, Napoleon, who organized many of the art galleries. Particularly in Germany and Austria, theaters and concert halls derive from princely courts and continue to receive state subsidies. Throughout Europe devotees of a given author still convene as "Friends of X" in order to function as courtly patrons. As we have seen, pseudocourtly patrons find it expedient to plan according to the calendar of anniversaries. The United States, by way of contrast, has no tradition of central control of culture to match that of Europe's former monarchies. The lack of courtly heritage is another reason why organizers in America feel less impelled to rely upon anniversaries as a means of coordinating activities.

Everyone can see that the cult of anniversaries enables contemporary nations to reknit ties with the past. In the postmodern era, craving for national identity impels governments to work harder to purvey a sense of roots. What is not so obvious is that the institutions through which Europe implements the cult of anniversaries are themselves throwbacks to the past. Europe's infrastructure for mounting commemorations perpetuates the very past it commemorates. The museums, academies, universities, writers' societies, and cultural ministries that sponsor anniversaries derive from initiatives of eighteenth- and nineteenth-century rulers. Often their successors exude an Old Regime aura, not just in the quarters they occupy, but in their modes of operation.

In Europe cultural civil servants perform functions that originated in princely courts. Of course, the audience being served no longer consists of a prince and his entourage but rather a democratic public nurtured on electronic media and the mass press. Cultural civil servants are courtiers who serve a general public. In the United States, on the other hand, courtly tradition never existed. Cultural practices derive from commerce, and managers are entrepreneurs or hucksters rather than courtiers. Often they lack the polish that comes from having grown up amidst age-old etiquette. Business firms and universities can hardly hope to boost national identity where the government declines to do so. If European cultural anniversaries retain a courtly air, American ones exude a prosaic one. Where Europeans value atmosphere, Americans value output, and cultural anniversaries require nothing so much as atmosphere.

Europe's Courtly Apparatus and Its Devotion to the Great Calendar

The resemblance of cultural managers in Europe to courtly officials embraces a variety of attitudes, the most important of which is veneration for the Great Calendar. As we have seen, the civil servants who staff museums, libraries, academies, writers' organizations, and cultural institutes play roles that evolved at princely courts. The relatively low pay, august settings, and opportunities to frequent notables all smack of courtly tradition. Moreover, the kind of entertainment that managers furnish the middle classes resembles what courtiers would have offered to princes in the eighteenth century. Concerts, exhibitions, lectures, and receptions abound in Europe's palaces today as they always have. Even television with its round-table discussions, theater performances, concerts, and films about notables has not significantly enlarged the repertoire of courtly amusement. Although the range of offerings has not expanded much since the time of Louis XV and Frederick the Great, the audiences have. The people, like yesterday's princes, want the latest and the showiest in music, literature, and art.

Europe's courtly apparatus can resist the trivialization of culture more resolutely than can America's twin infrastructures of mass entertainment and academic life. In Europe the cult of anniversaries does its part to help cultural managers combat the crasser expectations of the public. Among intellectuals the cult of anniversaries ensures that antidemocratic figures like Hobbes, Eichendorff, Pater, and Barbey d'Aurevilly will get a modicum of attention. Thinkers who devoted their careers to denouncing democratization get commemorated along with prophets of mass culture. This cannot happen in the United States, as the neglect of Henry Adams in 1988 and James Fenimore Cooper in 1989 showed. Antidemocrats contribute to the national identity of Europeans in a way that they do not in the United States.

The Great Calendar plays a special role in connecting Europe's cultural managers with their courtly predecessors. Managers welcome the dictates of the calendar because it removes any temptation to quarrel about fundamentals. By allowing the calendar to supply an agenda for each year, managers can implement that agenda without having to face issues of principle that might destroy consensus. The Great Calendar prevents quarrels about the court schedule. The courtier-managers defer to the Great Calendar as they would to a sovereign, knowing that their counterparts all over Europe serve the same master. The roster of anniversaries functions like a benevolent monarch whose will is law. What Americans might decry as subservience to a despot can be defended as courtier's tact, for in practice, the Great Calendar, no less than the Roman Catholic church, admits of many deviations. Local exceptions abound under the aegis of the Schedule-Maker-in-the-Sky.

Besides helping managers to coordinate endeavors, the Great Calendar facilitates publicity as well. By providing a rationale for each season's offerings, it furnishes a backdrop of consensus against which publicity can thrive. In today's Europe, it is no more necessary to justify an anniversary than it is to defend a national holiday, for both belong to the "natural" order of things. The analogy between the cult of anniversaries and traditions of monarchy runs even deeper. Just as no human contrivance determines when monarchs get born, reign, and die, so no planners have selected the birth or death years of cultural luminaries. In countries that retain or have once known monarchies (and this means all of Europe), the arbitrariness, or as existentialists would say the "thrownness," of cultural anniversaries is accepted with the same aplomb as is the birth and death of members of a royal family. No one pretends that such matters can be scheduled the way the election of officials is in the United States. Anniversaries invoke family, church, and the soil — things that grow organically rather than things built on command. The civil servants who manage anniversaries mediate between the rhythms of nature and the demands of consumers. Enveloped in age-old etiquette, courtier-managers personify organic growth in an age that otherwise exalts industrialism.

The cult of anniversaries recalls earlier generations' dependence on the life and death of dynasties. Until World War I, European history was shaped by accidents of birth and death among royalty. To give just one example, the throat cancer that killed the German Emperor Frederick III after 100 days of rule in 1888 and brought his brother Wilhelm II to the throne changed the course of history, probably not for the better. Although democratic countries no longer like to recall the illness of monarchs, they do romanticize calamities that befell creators. The illness that felled Lord Byron at Missolonghi, or the incapacity of Nietzsche during his last eleven years, or the motorcycle accident that killed T.E. Lawrence constitute part of their legend. Such mischances humanize giants.

Now that writers, artists, and musicians have replaced kings and queens as carriers of national identity, courtiers of culture marshal favorites according to rules of fate as arbitrary as those of heraldry. Courtiers have always liked arbitrary criteria such as titles confer. What wins a slot in the court calendar today is not so much what a creator accomplished as the year in which he was born or died. That way planners cannot be accused of pushing personal favorites. Today's cultural managers invoke accidents of birth and death the way a master of ceremonies might have invoked titles in the eighteenth century, robbing decisions about precedence of all acrimony.

The cohort of celebrands in a given year can be likened to a king's guests, who receive a royal welcome for a year and then return to oblivion. The dismissal of last year's darlings may seem callous, but it accords with the attitude of courts toward fallen favorites. The lion of the day takes all the applause. European cultural managers may be accused not so much of pandering to commercialism as of bowing to the whims of the Great Calendar. Creators whose birth and death anniversaries fall outside the present decade get ignored, while a given year's guests get adulated. The hospitality of kings is notoriously fickle.

By a strange twist, European television has intensified the grip of the Great Calendar. Television and radio seize upon each year's roster of celebrands to facilitate cultural programming. Films, concerts, symposia, and talk shows honor the celebrands as though they were princes for a year. However obsequious, the fawning of press agents, programmers, journalists, and professors fulfills a necessary function. In an age when hardly anyone agrees about fundamental values, everyone heeds the Schedule-Maker-in-the-Sky. By acquiescing in the cult of anniversaries, intellectuals exalt a technique of scheduling as a substitute for weightier consensus. Where people agree on little else, they welcome any source of assent, be it ever so innocuous.

In honoring distinguished citizens, France retains a not so innocuous custom from the Revolution: exhumation and transfer of bodies to the Pantheon. The exhumation and reburial of the economist Jean Monnet on his 100th birthday November 9, 1988, continued a practice that began during the first phase of the French Revolution. When the legislator Mirabeau died in the spring of 1791, the National Assembly voted to convert the newly completed Church of Sainte-Geneviève into a national Pantheon, to which they transferred the remains of Voltaire and Mirabeau during that year. Rousseau was reburied here in late 1794, and both he and Voltaire still lie in provisional wooden tombs of the period.[11]

Although the practice of exhumation derived from the Catholic church's reburial of saints in parish churches, it gave rise to outrages. During the Reign of Terror in 1793 the corpse of Cardinal de Richelieu was exhumed from his tomb in the chapel of the Sorbonne and publicly decapitated. His head was solemnly returned only in 1866. Even more macabre, on August 6–8, 1793, the tombs of the kings of France at the Abbey of Saint-Denis were opened, and during two weeks in October the bodies were thrown into two mass graves, one for the Bourbons and one for the Valois.[12] This desecration was intended to "celebrate" the first anniversary of the overthrow of monarchy (on August 10, 1792). Likewise in 1793 the remains of the fifth-century nun Sainte Geneviève, the patroness of Paris, were publicly burned and then thrown into the Seine. Resort to exhumation could cut both ways, however. After the fall of the Jacobins, the body of Mirabeau was removed from the Pantheon because his royalist conniving had been uncovered. He was replaced in late 1794 by Jean-Paul Marat, whose body was removed a few months later when the building was restored as a church. Such transfers occurred often enough to inspire a verb that may deserve revival: "to depantheonize" is to banish from commemoration.

When the Fifth Republic commemorated the centennial of Jean Monnet by transferring his bones to the Pantheon, the regime was perpetuating a ritual that derived not only from the Jacobins but also from courtly culture. Nearly every court in eighteenth-century Europe featured a burial crypt to house members of the royal family. The Kapuziner-Gruft in Vienna, the Theatiner-Gruft in Munich, and the church of Saint-Denis in Paris preserved the earthly remains of entire dynasties, including their cousins and their aunts. By reserving the Pantheon for heroes of republican civil religion, the revolutionaries replaced a royal crypt with a burial chapel for prestigious commoners.

The French Fifth Republic sponsors a democratized version of a royal crypt in order to honor favorite sons. As a climax to the bicentennial of the French Revolution, President Mitterand ordered the remains of the mathematician Gaspard Monge (1746–1818) transferred to the Pantheon along with those of a republican priest, the Abbé Grégoire, who had led the so-called constitutional church that had served the Revolution. As early as January 1794, the Abbé Grégoire coined the word *vandalism* to denounce Jacobin desecration not of corpses but of art monuments. He named such "killing the thing" after a Germanic tribe renowned for having ravaged Roman civilization in the fifth century.[13] His "pantheonization" unfolded with all possible pomp on December 12, 1989, although the Abbé Grégoire was so controversial that the Archbishop of Paris refused to take part.[14] The body of an advocate of universal education, the Marquis de Condorcet (1743–1794), would have shared the occasion if it had not disappeared into a common grave in 1794.[15] Willingness to move tombs is still another way in which democratic Europe perpetuates courtly etiquette. During the bicentennial no one seemed to care that since 1986 the nave of the Pantheon has been closed for structural repairs, so that only the crypt—it is after all the building's functional part—can be visited. As an ironic postscript, in February 1990 a court in Brussels forbade the transfer to Paris of the remains of the painter Jacques-

Louis David, who died in exile in 1825. His tomb has become a national treasure of the Belgians.

The United States lacks any equivalent of Europe's courtier-managers. There being no nationwide or even statewide ministries of culture, it falls to universities to undertake anniversary commemorations, particularly for cultural figures. For better or for worse, American academics resemble not so much courtiers as business entrepreneurs. Although a wide public attends university functions, citizens at large take little or no part in planning them. Because commemorations are so academic, the United States enjoys one advantage: it stands alone in the attention it can lavish on foreign celebrands. The immigrant background of America shows in its eagerness to commemorate British, French, German, and Italian heroes. The bicentennial of the French Revolution, for example, inspired two cities, Chicago and Houston, to mount outdoor celebrations, which included more than fifty events in Illinois financed by the Sara Lee Corporation.[16] Not to be outdone, academics staged an outpouring of conferences, exhibitions, and films, at among other institutions, New York University, the University of California at Los Angeles, and Georgetown University (which was concurrently celebrating its own bicentennial). As in France, themes from the French Revolution incited specialists in the United States to explore interdisciplinary issues. Although anniversaries of fellow Americans like Henry Adams and James Fenimore Cooper did not inspire scholars to transcend their specialties, that of the French Revolution did.

In similar fashion two conferences held at William and Mary College and at George Washington University in early 1989 on the 300th anniversary of the Accession of William and Mary galvanized American academics out of their specialism more conspicuously than did purely American anniversaries. European anniversaries provide American academics an opportunity to mingle across disciplinary lines. During 1989 anniversaries of European thinkers like Montesquieu, Freud, and Wittgenstein stimulated Americans to probe fundamental issues more effectively than did those of native-born C.S. Pierce (1839–1914), Henry George (1839–1897), or Walter Lippmann (1889–1974).

Many American academics continue to venerate a pantheon of European thinkers, whose insights enhance American self-scrutiny. One task of cultural anniversaries in American universities is to sustain European traditions of political reflection. English political theorists like Hobbes, Locke, and Burke, or French ones like Montesquieu, Rousseau, and Tocqueville raise fundamental issues that native theorists seldom had to confront. American scholars of conservative bent still depend on European tradition to furnish their tutelary thinkers. Of course, only universities can commemorate these mentors, whose ideas remain unknown to the people at large. American intellectuals seldom discuss Rousseau and Tocqueville, or even Jefferson and Lincoln, on television the way French ones do. Anniversaries connect Europeans to their courtly past in palpable and public ways, while American universities honor Europe's courtly heritage in self-imposed detachment. While the French and the Germans parade their traditions of courtly and revolutionary anniversaries, American academics have yet to forge a style for presenting luminaries to a larger audience. The separation of church and state lives on in a separation of university and public.

Notes

1. Thomas Mann wrote a novel on this theme, *Lotte in Weimar* (Stockholm: Bermann-Fischer, 1939), translated as *The Beloved Returns* (New York: Knopf, 1940).
2. Jerrold Seigel, *Bohemian Paris: Culture, Politics, and the Boundaries of Bourgeois Life, 1830–1930* (New York: Penguin, 1987).
3. For an analysis of Antonio Gramsci's concept of hegemony, see T.J. Jackson Lears, "The Concept of Cultural Hegemony: Problems and Possibilities," *American Historical Review*, 90 (1988): 567–593.
4. Reprinted from *Système de politique positive*, vol. 4 (Paris, 1854) in Gertrud Lenzer, ed., *Auguste Comte and Positivism: The Essential Writings* (New York: Harper and Row, 1975), pp. 472–473.
5. Joseph C. Sloane, *Paul Marc Joseph Chenavard, Artist of 1848* (Chapel Hill: University of North Carolina Press, 1962).
6. Claudine Mitchell, "Time and the Idea of Patriarchy in the Pastorals of Puvis de Chavannes," *Art History*, 10 (1987): 188–202.
7. Exhibition Catalog, *The Treasure Houses of Britain* (Washington, D.C.: The National Gallery of Art, 1986).
8. Pascal Ory, *Les Expositions universelles de Paris: panorama raisonné* (Paris: Ramsay, 1982); Werner Hofmann, *The Earthly Paradise: Art in the Nineteenth Century* (New York: Braziller, 1961), pp. 165–198.
9. The home of Edith Wharton in Lenox, Massachusetts, built about 1900, hosts Shakespeare performances as though it were an aristocratic domain.

10. Peter Bergmann, *Nietzsche: The Last Apolitical German* (Bloomington: Indiana University Press, 1986), pp. 21–23, which cites Alex Gehring, *Genie und Verehrergemeinde* (Bonn, 1968). A penetrating analysis of German usages is Harold James, *A German Identity, 1770–1990* (New York: Routledge, 1989).

11. Mona Ozouf "Le Panthéon: L'École Normale des morts," in Pierre Nora, ed., *Les Lieux de mémoire*, vol. I, *La République* (Paris: Gallimard, 1984), pp. 139–166.

12. Emmet Kennedy, *A Cultural History of the French Revolution* (New Haven: Yale University Press, 1989), pp. 206–212.

13. Bronislaw Baczko, "Vandalism," in Furet and Ozouf, eds., *A Critical Dictionary of the French Revolution* (Cambridge: Harvard University Press, 1989), pp. 860–868.

14. A polemic against the Abbé Grégoire in Jean Dumont, *La Révolution française ou les prodiges du sacrilège* (Limoges: Criterion, 1984), pp. 358–425, raises many doubts about the revolutionary bishop, who was a better propagandist than churchman. Pantheonization tended to stifle debate about his merits.

15. Condorcet's revolutionary zeal is examined in Renée Winegarten, "Visions of Elysium: Condorcet: Liberal or Revolutionary?" *Encounter*, 74 (January 1990): 24–33.

16. Bertrand Le Gendre, "US gets authentic taste of Revolution — French style," *Manchester Guardian Weekly* (May 7, 1989), p. 16.

6

Humanist Tradition as a Link between Countries and Generations

The Cultural Religion of Humanism and the Cult of Anniversaries in Europe

The deeper one looks at the cult of anniversaries, the more it discloses about differences between Europe and the United States. Divergences in the roles of civil religion, the commemoration industry, and courtly traditions do not exhaust differences between the two continents' cultural styles. Perhaps one reason why no one has studied the phenomenon of anniversaries in today's world is that the cultural divide across the Atlantic upsets any theory that seeks to encompass both approaches. Americans, who deplore the commercializing of their own culture, tend to see Europe's cult of anniversaries as a marketing device, while Europeans tend to overlook American commemorations because they omit cultural heroes. This chapter explores in greater depth certain assumptions about commemorating creators that European countries share with one another in contrast to the United States.

Americans commemorate events, Europeans commemorate creators. Behind their cult of cultural luminaries, Europeans uphold a version of the Great Man Theory of History. In keeping with humanist beliefs that have flourished since the fourteenth century, Europeans adulate creative geniuses. Each year's celebrands form links in a Golden Chain of Genius that connects the 1990s with generations who have honored the same figures stretching back to Dante, Boccaccio, and Petrarch in the 1300s. The cult of anniversaries renews the humanist chain with a fresh round of honorees each year.

Americans' celebration of events rests on a different assumption, which has become known as the Whig view of history. As the English historian Herbert Butterfield explained in 1931, proponents of the Whig view hail those events and figures that abet progress and deride those that uphold stability or provoke decline.[1] American commemorations celebrate events that advanced progress, however awkward that may be to define. The nation's bicentennial in 1976, the bicentennial of the Constitution in 1987, the centennials of individual states, and the anniversaries of cities and towns all proclaim improvement in the economy and or in government. Even the Civil War during its centennial between 1961 and 1965, as well as its 125th anniversary between 1986 and 1990, got saluted for having ended the scourge of slavery. A sadder kind of commemoration has crept in since the assassination of President Kennedy in 1963. Although his death, coupled with the waste of the Vietnam war, called into question the Whig view of history, most Americans cannot commemorate their past without invoking a progressive view of it. President Kennedy is mourned for having launched an unfinished agenda of progressive measures. American civil religion imposes faith in the progress of American institutions.

Europeans harbor no such faith in the upward course of history. They need not demonstrate that a creator advanced human or national well-being in order to honor him. The humanist tradition asks only that a creator have produced works that delight sensibility or enlarge wisdom. An artist or a writer need not have prodded history forward in order to join the Golden Stream of Genius. To illustrate the difference between the two assumptions, let us take an American like Henry Adams (1838–1918).[2] A dyspeptic of his originality, who excelled as a critic of modernization, would get amply commemorated in any European country. But because he rejected much of America's civil religion, including faith in progress and in industrialism, Adams is regarded with suspicion and even disdain. Progressives regard him as a disillusioned provincial who misunderstood a booming continent. Whereas Europeans would salute Adams for having proposed an alternative view of the course of history, Americans relegate him to the status of maverick. A critic of America's civil religion finds no place in the national pantheon the way such outsiders do in France or Germany.

The humanist tradition predates the emergence of nation-states. Because its origins are transnational, it offers a vision of excellence that sidesteps the issue of nationality. At the same time as the cult of anniversaries promotes national identity, European humanism discourages exclusive preoccupation with it. The humanist tradition places its honorees in a dual light: they are exalted both as panhuman geniuses and as national (or local) heroes. By a strange twist, European anniversaries, although they are financed from national budgets, lift their celebrands out of a national limelight into a broader context. Links in the Golden Chain of Genius outsoar any one nation's claim to greatness.

The United States seems to prefer a Golden Chain of Founders. One symptom of parochialism in commemorations is Americans' reluctance to interpret cultural figures in a transnational context. Henry Adams would grow in stature if he were aligned not just with American contemporaries like the Social Darwinists William Graham Sumner or Lester Ward, but with European philosophers of history like Hippolyte Taine or Wilhelm Dilthey. Against the backdrop of American progressivism Adams appears eccentric, while against the backdrop of European *fin-de-siècle* despair he appears strangely optimistic. His voice belongs among those of Europe's seers, not among America's boosters. For Americans to adopt humanist assumptions would open new possibilities for commemorations. Intellectuals due for commemoration, like Benjamin Franklin in 1990 and Thomas Jefferson in 1993, would emerge in a new light if they could be interpreted as Europeanized sages instead of as American progressives.

As differences in the cult of anniversaries show, most Americans have lost touch with European humanism. Among American scholars of the humanities, post-1960 trends like structuralism and deconstruction have severed ties to older traditions of learning. Among Europeans, however, the rise of iconoclastic methodologies has not weakened the cult of anniversaries as a vehicle of humanism. Whereas many American scholars have embraced new methodologies to the exclusion of the old—after all this seems the progressive thing to do—Europeans have inserted the novelties into the Golden Chain of Genius as only the latest in a centuries-old stream of innovation. The cult of anniversaries helps Europeans to keep sane about the latest fashions.

The Golden Chain of Genius, stretching back through the Renaissance and Middle Ages to antiquity, imparts to European civilization much of its distinctiveness. Shared memories of founders like Charlemagne and Saint Bernard of Clairvaux and of seers like Dante and Montaigne connect Europeans to a common heritage. If Europeans were to scuttle the Golden Chain, their history would fall apart into a tale of warring tribes. At a time when European economies and nation-states are interlocking more than ever before, anniversaries of pan-European figures nourish the very idea of Europe. European identity, as a capstone to national identity, rests not least upon memories of cultural heroes. Now more than ever, integration of the European Community encourages commemorating pan-European luminaries.

In honoring each year's crop of anniversaries, the French, Germans, Austrians, Italians, and British celebrate their heritage as Europeans, not just as patriots. Although financed by national and local governments, the cult of anniversaries promotes European unity as well. This applies particularly to cultural figures who emerged before the Renaissance. Writers, artists, and churchmen from antiquity and the Middle Ages belong to all of Europe, not just to the region that nurtured them. Homer, Socrates, and Virgil, no less than Saint Augustine, Saint Benedict, and Saint Thomas Aquinas are universal figures who personify pan-European heritage.

If we look beyond the quality of celebrands to assess their quantity, the message is the same. Even allowing for differences of opinion about who deserves attention, starting about 600 B.C. in ancient Greece and running to the tenth century A.D., many dozens of names emerge in each century as worthy of commemoration. From the eleventh century on, the number of potential honorees in each century swells into the hundreds, and after about 1600, into the thousands. The fecundity of Europe in notable men and women is perhaps its supreme mark of distinction. The scope, creativity, and diversity of these creators places Europe in a class by itself. Functioning as a modern substitute for the cult of ancestors, the cult of anniversaries rotates a fresh group of names before the public each year. In view of the tens of thousands of Europeans who invite remembrance, each year's crop of somewhere between fifty and a hundred active honorees seems but a drop in the ocean.[3]

The countries of Europe share a cult of luminaries that binds the continent together much the way America's civil religion does the United States. Whereas America's civil religion celebrates ideals of toleration, progress, and social mobility, Europe's cult of luminaries exalts rather different ones: creativity, versatility, and genius. Perhaps one should speak of a European cultural religion that functions as a counterpart to America's civil religion. This transnational religion of culture sustains European identity by honoring creators for accomplishments that benefited mankind. Europe's cultural religion honors individual vision, one-of-a-kind breakthroughs, and one-man accomplishments, whereas America's civil religion, as Tocqueville observed in the 1830s, values a middlingness that binds the nation together.[4] The American nation cannot identify with mavericks like Henry Adams or Henry James.

The cult of anniversaries nourishes Europe's religion of culture by inspiring commemorations of pan-European import. Even when a town is celebrating its hero, everyone is aware what role he played on a larger stage. The disproportion between local fervor and world fame looms largest in Italy. In 1983 the town of Urbino commemorated Raphael as a native son at a time when museums throughout Europe and the United States were celebrating him as perhaps the most influential of all painters. In 1987 the town of Cremona celebrated the 250th anniversary of the death of the violin-maker Antonio Stradivari (c. 1644–1737), knowing that every violinist throughout the world would wish to own one of his creations. In 1988 the city of Milan commemorated the 250th anniversary of the jurist Cesare Beccaria (1738–1794), whose book *On Crimes and Punishments* (1764) advocated reforms of penal law that have benefited all mankind. Anniversaries encourage communities to assert the local ties of universal figures. By grounding a universal benefactor in his roots, an anniversary humanizes him in much the way that Renaissance images of the Madonna and Child humanized the figure of Christ. Local commemorations bring a titanic creator back to earth, and by making a giant seem universal, they also enhance European identity.

Some anniversary commemorations assert the hallowedness of places through the ages. The electronic media tend to homogenize places; television, telephones, and fax machines blend places into a blur of ubiquity. By fostering the illusion that a viewer can be in many places at once, electronic media diminish awe at the here and now. Certain commemorations combat the leveling of places by heightening awareness that each place is unique. Certain anniversaries exalt *genius loci*. In 1989, for example, the Great Saint Bernard Pass across the Alps between France and Italy marked the 2000th anniversary of its opening by the Romans in 12 B.C. Local promoters mounted celebrations along the way between Martigny in Switzerland and Aosta in Italy. A new museum opened, treks over the pass abounded, and medieval festivities unfolded, bringing into focus two millennia of triumph over weather, altitude, and remoteness. Visitors learned that although since about 1050 Augustinian canons had run a hospice there in the name of Saint Bernard of Aosta (923–1008), they did not introduce the celebrated dogs until the nineteenth century. While international media paid little attention, throughout the summer the place exuded its aura for the benefit of any who happened to pass through. Such anniversaries combat leveling by the electronic media, even as others like the French Revolutionary bicentennial reinforce it.

The cult of anniversaries in Europe invokes a panorama of creativity that stretches across more than two thousand five hundred years. This Golden Chain encompasses a truly dazzling variety of cultures. It honors followers of three world religions (Judaism, Christianity, Islam), as well as countless sects within these; it embraces speakers of several dozen major languages, in addition to hundreds of dialects within them; and it includes citizens of hundreds of cities and towns, each of which maintains libraries, museums, or other forums of collective memory. At a time when subnational regions and ethnic groups are trumpeting their particularity, the cult of anniversaries exalts transnational creators who enlarged the idea of Europe. By honoring the places in which they flourished, Europe honors itself. If antihumanists were to abolish the cult of anniversaries, another way would have to be found to remind Europeans of their distinctiveness. An abundance of creative geniuses is what sets European civilization apart from all others. European nations practice the cult of anniversaries not just because *homo rhythmicus* needs holidays or because the commemoration industry needs agendas but because Europeans need emblems of uniqueness. The cult of anniversaries nurtures a cultural religion that worships genius. Through the rituals of that religion Europe rehearses its inner unity.

Using Anniversaries to Bridge the Generation Gap

Insofar as the cult of anniversaries involves venerating ancestors, its practitioners have an obligation to initiate each new generation into the Golden Stream. Anniversary commemorations ought to woo the attention of young people to each year's crop of worthies. Experience shows that this is easier to do for events than for creators. During 1989, for example, the city of Paris drew the attention of children to the French Revolution through devices such as "Find-the-Treasure" games, art contests, and tours of revolutionary sites. Many of the activities scheduled in Paris during the summer of 1989 were designed specifically for adolescents and young adults, including rock concerts, street dancing, and open-air films, which it was felt would attract youth more strongly than do theater, light-and-sound shows, or the inevitable fireworks. Even so, children and adolescents became more quickly surfeited than adults, and everyone suffered from bicentennial overkill.

Indeed, cultural anniversaries tend to interest adults more than young people. Europe's courtier-managers seem to have forgotten that secondary schools no longer initiate middle-class teenagers into the Golden Stream of Creativity. Europeans presently enrolled in university have not absorbed the cult of luminaries the way their parents did. Moreover, children find the timing of anniversaries arbitrary. Oblivious to the weight of centuries, they do not experience the same need for festivities to mark one's place in the calendar. Why should adults suddenly be talking about the French Revolution in 1989 but not in 1987 or 1991? From a child's point-of-view, historical fads seem to come and go without reference to abiding values. Those young people who discern the hollowness at the core of postmodernism might welcome acknowledgment that the cult of anniversaries rests on lack of any deeper consensus. Once skepticism about excessive reliance on the Great Calendar has subsided, certain anniversaries could be planned with the concerns of young adults expressly in mind. Each year certain figures should be selected from the crop of celebrands for marketing to students. Creators who themselves were young or who wrote in a youthful vein cry out to be rejuvenated.

This task is harder than it seems because few of Europe's creators strove to appeal to youth. Most celebrands address people who are middle-aged or older. There are, to be sure, a few obvious exceptions. In 1990 the dandy Beau Brummell (1778–1840) and the Alpinist Edward Whymper (1840–1911) could have been celebrated as exemplars of youthful energy, however diversely expressed. In 1991 the English poet of youthful dalliance Robert Herrick (1591–1674) and the French poet of youthful self-destruction Arthur Rimbaud

(1854–1891) can be commemorated together as bards of youthful vagary. Herrick's advice "To gather your rosebuds while ye may" can be applied to Rimbaud's hallucinogenic quest. In 1992 the English prodigy Percy Bysshe Shelley (1792–1822) and the writer of fantasy J.R.R. Tolkien (1892–1973) could be commemorated as fellow visionaries. The same might be done in 1993 with the young playwright Christopher Marlowe (1564–1593) and the German idealist poet Friedrich Hölderlin (1770–1843). Marlowe's death in a tavern brawl at age 29 compares with Hölderlin's mental breakdown in 1802. These champions and eventual victims of youthful brio can be presented both as models and warnings to today's young people.

The message should be that not all creators were middle-aged pontificators. All too often, Europe's cult of anniversaries exalts figures whom young people reject. In reaction partly against the French Revolution, since 1815 both French and German culture have idolized old men: Goethe is honored for late works like the second part of *Faust* (1832) more than for youthful ones like *The Sorrows of Young Werther* (1774). The centennial in 1985 of Victor Hugo honored him as the middle-aged critic of Napoleon III who wrote *Les Misérables* (1862) rather than as the youthful daredevil who wrote *Hernani* (1830). So to enshrine the aged is to cripple youth. Too often to exalt Goethe has meant to endow him with a superhuman aura that stifles rather than stimulates. Indeed, from his fate one could fashion a verb to denote a tendency to exile giants to Olympus: to make geniuses seem unattainable is to "goethify" them.

To goethify past creators is to elevate them beyond any hope of imitation. Nostalgia can extend to lamenting that genuine creativity has perished, never to be recovered, so that we survivors are condemned to admire a past we cannot hope to emulate. Such paralysis afflicted Germany in the decades after the death of Goethe and contributed to the rise of the cult of anniversaries. In the 1830s and 1840s Germans thought of themselves as passé because giants like Goethe, Hegel, and Beethoven had died. If commemorations are to excite young people, planners must scrap any notion of goethifying the celebrands. Mourning a lost past must give way to welcoming the future.

A danger in the opposite direction lies in trivializing creators so that they begin to resemble rock stars or movie idols. This approach can be called "disneyfying" the past, in recognition of techniques exploited at Disneyland and the like. At these emporiums of replicas, sanitizing the past involves removing any cause of offense to the point of shrinking buildings to three-quarters their original size. By prettifying, diminishing, and simplifying the past, disneyfiers deny any difference between us and the great creators. The latter emerge as uncles who could have lived next door. American television abounds in this kind of popularization. Young people need commemorations that neither distance nor trivialize creators but rather present them as having experienced in their own time dilemmas similar to those of today.

Efforts to imbue commemorations with youthful verve will show that many cultural figures resist such doctoring. Certain thinkers deserve to be commemorated for the wisdom of old age rather than for youthful bravado. French tradition abounds in such sages. Among those coming up during the early 1990s will be the philosopher Henri Bergson (1859–1941), the historian of religion Ernest Renan (1823–1892), and the cultural historian Hippolyte Taine (1828–1893). These savants elaborated a wisdom of old age that ought to be proclaimed as such. Commemorators might even emphasize critiques of heedless youth in favor of the ripeness of old age. Taine in particular believed that youth should emulate not their peers but their grandparents. France also produced cynical writers who never prized carefree youth: among those soon to be commemorated are the Marquis de Sade (1740–1814), Guy de Maupassant (1850–1893), and Céline (1894–1961). Far from being construed as exponents of youth, they should be exposed as nonbelievers in it. These cynics did not believe in personal growth and have scant appeal for those who do.

The question of how to package youthful thinkers for youths and adult thinkers for adults raises a thorny issue. Some thinkers of note enjoy almost no recognition in today's world. How should programmers handle figures who deserve attention but are unlikely to win it? The problem pertains particularly to lay religious writers. Germany in the late eighteenth century, for example, produced brilliant lay mystics who influenced many other writers but have never been revived since then. Johann Heinrich Jung-Stilling (1740–1817) expounded Lutheran pietism in his autobiography (1777), Friedrich Heinrich Jacobi (1743–1819) anticipated Christian existentialism and invented the term *nihilism*, and Franz von Baader (1765–1841) as a lay Catholic taught the protestant notion of God's unfolding through human self-development *(Bildung)*.

These were dedicated, productive, and ingenious thinkers who in our ecumenical age deserve a wider public than they are ever likely to find. The cult of anniversaries, with its emphasis on promoting national or local identity and on sustaining courtly traditions amid a commemoration industry, has no truck with mystical thinkers. Arguably such figures deserve commemoration, at least in their hometowns, but their preference for spirituality over national identity makes them ill-suited to attract resources. Just as a sage like Renan bores youth, and a youth like Shelley exasperates the aged, so mystics repel the courtier-managers who schedule commemorations. Anniversaries will become a comprehensive medium of discourse only when sponsors aspire to create a public for significant thinkers who as yet have none.

The lack of popularity of certain celebrands underlines a larger truth. Even if marginal figures get ignored, Europeans mount a breathtaking array of commemorations each year. Compared to the paucity of cultural figures who get commemorated in the United States, the variety and brilliance of Europe's commemorations dazzles the beholder. Each year European culture places its fecundity on display through conferences, exhibitions, films, and talk shows dedicated to anniversary occasions. Even if planners do too little to attract youth, the panorama of emulatable figures remains astonishing.

Willingness each year to commemorate up to a hundred creators in a dozen countries is ushering in something like a Common Market in Culture within the European Economic Community. Anniversaries have become the common coin of a transnational market in culture. Because courtier-managers throughout Europe share common values, travelers know what sort of exhibitions, lectures, reenactments, and films to expect wherever they go. Each year's anniversaries throw up fresh luminaries and events for Europeans to incorporate into their identity. Year after year the offerings reinforce an image of Europe as a continent that for more than two dozen centuries has never lacked innovators.

Although the great powers of anniversaries (France, Germany, Austria, Italy, and Britain) boast a more nearly unbroken stream of creativity than do, say, Scandinavia or Portugal or Poland, the radiance embraces all of Europe. Anniversaries nourish Europe's self-image as the world's preeminent seedbed of invention. They promote a European-wide awareness of shared values supported by shared heroes. Commemorations financed by national and regional agencies build a

European identity as effectively as they do a national and regional one. The Common Market in anniversaries does its part to buttress the Common Market in commodities. Pan-European consciousness gets strengthened each year through the proliferation of anniversaries. Part Two of this book will explore ways in which this commonality can foster new attitudes as the bimillennium approaches.

Notes

1. Herbert Butterfield, *The Whig Interpretation of History* (London: Bell, 1931). On the emergence of belief in progress see David Spadafora, *The Idea of Progress in Eighteenth-Century Britain* (New Haven: Yale University Press, 1990).
2. Ernest Samuels, *Henry Adams* (Cambridge: Harvard University Press, 1989).
3. J.O. Thorne, ed., *Chambers's Biographical Dictionary*, rev. ed. (New York: St Martin's Press, 1974) contains over 15,000 entries on notable Europeans and Americans.
4. The decline in popularity since the 1950s of Alexis de Tocqueville, *De la démocratie en Amérique* (Paris, 1835–1840) indicates a reluctance to face his criticisms of American middlingness. The 150th anniversary of the book in 1985 met less acclaim than did the 100th of his birth in 1959. For a reassessment, see André Jardin, *Tocqueville: A Biography* (New York: Farrar, Straus and Giroux, 1988), translated from *Alexis de Tocqueville, 1805–1859* (Paris: Hachette, 1984).

7

Objections to the Cult of Anniversaries

How Do Humans Interact with Nature?
The Greek and the Structuralist View

So far this book has celebrated the cult of anniversaries. Only rarely has it referred to objections that cynics mount against the commercialization of anniversaries. The time has come to examine fundamental objections to the cult of anniversaries. In order to understand the appeal and nonappeal of anniversaries, it helps to place them in a context beyond national identity, commercial exploitation, courtly tradition, and contrasts between Europe and the United States. Anniversaries arise because human beings get born at a time and in a place not of anyone's choosing. Through their very arbitrariness, anniversaries remind us of our thrownness as creatures. They recall the cycle of nature that decrees that creatures must be born, mature, and die. Through anniversaries, no less than through other rituals, humans acknowledge a transience that they strive to tame. One way to bear the transience of life is to institute a cult of fame that will outlive those who created it. The first part of this chapter examines ways in which, through different phases of history, the cult of commemorations has cast a shadow beyond the grave.

There are two ways of viewing anniversaries, or indeed any human institution: as having been made by humans or as having been imposed by nature. Some people assume that anniversaries are arbitrary, as patently man-made as the metric system or the concept of miles-per-hour. Others assume that to commemorate births and deaths is as "natural" as is the need to eat or to sleep. Since humans are born and die like other animals, to recall this fact integrates humans into a cycle not of conventions but of nature. Which view is correct? Are anniversaries human conventions, or are they intrusions of nature? Or are they both?

Anniversaries owe their fascination to the fact that humans have to accept certain realities imposed by the earth's revolving around the sun. Just as the seasons come and go, so do individual lives. Our calendar, our experience of the seasons, and our metaphors for the cycle of life reflect realities that no one made. The calendar, like the anniversaries that depend on it, is a human convention that imposes order on an ineluctable process. As Eviatar Zerubavel emphasizes, this man-made order imparts regularity to the flow of time. The calendar, incorporating a potential for celebrating anniversaries, domesticates our experience of the earth's revolution around the sun. Though man-made, these conventions have their roots in nature. At bottom, *homo rhythmicus* vibrates to rhythms of the cosmos.

The distinction between humans and nature underlies the vocabulary we use to talk about anniversaries. As pioneered by the ancient Greeks, Western thought, which is to say European thought, posited that humans stand apart from nature. From Homer down to the nineteenth century, Western culture inculcated a distinction between the human and the natural. Nature was defined as the realm that humans cannot alter. The weather, earthquakes, the sea, disease, and the like, exemplified forces of nature that challenge and ultimately subdue humans. The Greeks devised deities to symbolize these transhuman realms, while medieval Christianity branded them as dangerous or even hostile. Yet far from belittling humans, the ancient Greeks exalted their own ability to differentiate themselves from nature. In the Greek view, man evolved from within nature into a creature who stands apart from it. Art, science, and politics show that humans can devise institutions that protect them from nature and enable them to channel some of its constraints. As the Greeks discovered, medicine permits humans to live longer, technology permits them to build higher and travel farther, while philosophy permits them to understand their condition better than nature itself would seem to invite.

The notion that humans surpass other animals by using their minds to devise language underpins the view that in the fifteenth and sixteenth centuries became known as humanism. Western humanism, which flourished in ancient Greece and Rome and again from the fifteenth to the nineteenth centuries, interpreted human life as a contest unfolding between nature and mind. Western culture hinged on a byplay between nonhuman nature and man the maker and thinker. In grandiose fashion the German philosopher Hegel (1770–1831) climaxed this tradition by envisioning its byplay as an ongoing process in which humans transform nature into a hybrid realm that he called culture. Having begun enveloped by nature, humans have used their minds to transform the environment into culture, so that they no longer live menaced by nature but rather increasingly dominate it. Hegel's philosophy, devised at the start of the Biedermeier period, specified how successive peoples from the Egyptians, Greeks, and Romans onward have contributed to the process of transmuting nature into culture. In his *Phenomenology of Mind* (1807) and later works, Hegel heralded heroes like Sophocles, Archimedes, Gutenberg, and Luther, whose breakthroughs in shaping culture deserve commemorating.[1] Not a few of them constitute the staple of European anniversaries to this day.

A more subtle way to think about human emergence from nature is to suggest that human instincts, which originally bound us to nature, have altered under conditions of culture. Institutions have replaced raw instinct as a way of guiding behavior. If instinct is equated with nature, then institutions have supplanted ties to nature with those to man-made structures.[2] Either way, what anniversaries celebrate is mankind's long process of emergence from bondage to nature.

Two generations before Hegel, a nostalgic thinker like Jean-Jacques Rousseau (1712–1778) deplored the fact that humans were outgrowing intimacy with nature. Urging that instinct be cultivated, he advocated child-centered education, confessional writing, and walks in the country as ways to recover, however sporadically, a spontaneity that had been lost.[3] Although Rousseau knew that we cannot regress from culture back to nature, like many nostalgics today he rebuked as decadent those sophisticates whom he blamed for the loss. The heroes he would have preferred to commemorate presumably included artists and writers like himself, who kept alive the ideal of a shepherd's Arcadia as an alternative to instinct-stunting institutions. He was particularly fond of ancient ascetics like the Spartan lawgiver Lycurgus or the Roman farmer-soldier Cincinnatus, who today boast no public whatever. Rousseau's heroes offer scant promise for revival.

In the late twentieth century the views of both Rousseau and Hegel seem simplistic, not least because the notion of separation between humans and nature has taken on a new dimension. The German physicist Werner Heisenberg put the matter bluntly in 1958 when he argued that scientists can no longer "know" nature because the instruments by which they measure it alter the outcome.[4] In order to gain one bit of information, physicists must forego acquiring another. This notion generalizes Heisenberg's announcement in 1927 of the "Indeterminacy Principle," which held that in measuring the position and momentum of electrons, the act of measurement precludes measuring at the same instant energy expended and time elapsed. Even as we purport to know more about nature, the nature we claim to know gets altered by our intruding. Contrary to the Greeks and to Hegel, physicists believe that our explorations contaminate what we seek to investigate.

Physical evidence of the despoiling of nature abounds. Hikers in the wilderness breathe air contaminated by factories thousands of miles distant. The same hikers come upon plastic debris discarded by previous ones, and all of them suffer from a depleted ozone layer. Humans scatter waste products heedlessly, so that the globe scarcely boasts a refuge devoid of human traces. If the cult of anniversaries began as a way to celebrate human dominion over nature, environmentalists wish they could curb such dominion. Like Rousseau, they would prefer to commemorate not the conquerors of nature but its preservers. In their eyes, not Thomas Edison but John Muir (1838–1914), the patron of America's national parks, deserves a year of adulation. In 1988 the Sierra Club, but not the United States as a whole, solemnly feted his 150th anniversary. In 1990 at the centennial of Yosemite Park, all concerned got another chance to commemorate heroes of conservation.

Since the 1940s a different conception of human interaction with nature has emerged from the French structuralists. Led by the anthropologist Claude Lévi-Strauss, they abandoned the distinction between man and nature.[5] Arguing that humans cannot escape being embedded in nature, they interpreted culture as an outcome of cooperation between our endowment of intelligence and a particular civilization's physical environment. Primitive peoples collaborate with plants and animals in their habitat to devise a culture whose structures embody propensities inherent in mind. Whereas Hegel saw culture as transforming nature into something transnatural, Lévi-Strauss sees culture as consummating nature through application of another force of nature, namely mind. For the structuralists, mind penetrates nature in ways that are no less natural than those of Rousseau's instinct. Whereas the Greeks saw mind as opposing nature, the structuralists see mind as exemplifying it. Humans belong to nature, and culture emerges through a process of coping with nature from within.[6]

Denial of mind's transcendence over nature tends to diminish the appeal of cultural anniversaries, since luminaries are believed to exercise not unique gifts of spirit but rather natural capacities. Structuralists and poststructuralists, as represented by French savants like Lévi-Strauss, Michel Foucault, and Jacques Lacan, reprimand earlier Western tradition for having boasted about conquests of nature. Structuralists criticize humanist thinkers from Heraclitus to Sartre for arrogantly asserting that humans can "rise above" nature. Instead, these antitranscendentalists want to insert humans back into nature by tracing all human achievement to the "natural" functioning of our nervous systems. Humans are products of nature, who in creating culture have extended nature's domain instead of escaping it. Structuralists tend to deplore the cult of anniversaries for preaching false notions of human superiority to nature.

Whichever side one endorses in the debate between humanists and structuralists, it is clear that anniversaries address the issue of human interaction with nature. Anniversaries belong among the contrivances that humans have devised for coping with the transience of life. This function has to be performed in any culture, regardless of whether one regards culture as a conquest over nature or a collaboration with it. Whether willingly or not, structuralists have to abide today's proliferation of anniversaries because these help contemporaries to accept the cycle of birthing and dying.

In many societies, particularly non-Western ones, ceremonies stress annual repetition instead of periodic recurrences like 50th or 100th anniversaries. In primitive societies, the yearly cycle dictates rituals of food-gathering, child-rearing, and religion. Because each year is much like another, the emphasis at annual feasts falls on repetition, not singularity.[7] Celebrations affirm sameness rather than proclaim breakthroughs. Most primitive peoples share the structuralist conviction that society abides in unchanging nature. Because such cyclical cultures lack a notion of innovation, they celebrate annual anniversaries in order to affirm routine rather than to herald change. The cult of breakthroughs emerged later.

Ancient Greece and Rome favored religious festivals that ratified the unchanging cycle of the years. But in addition, they instituted a framework for honoring never-to-be-repeated achievements of individuals. The Olympic Games, which began at Olympia in 776 B.C. and continued every four years (with interruptions) until A.D. 393, convened athletes from all over Greece to compete for immortal fame. Already by the sixth century B.C., poets were celebrating the accomplishments of each new round of champions. The Athenian lyric poet Pindar (522/518–c. 438) devoted his odes to commemorating the heroes of these and other pan-Hellenic contests. Just as Pindar aspired to confer immortality on feats of athletic prowess, so the historian Herodotus immortalized those Athenians who, against overwhelming odds, had defeated the Persians at Marathon in 490 B.C. Like the Olympic champions, these soldiers had surmounted constraints of nature, and for this they were extolled. Admiration for once-in-a-lifetime breakthroughs lies at the heart of the cult of anniversaries.

Commemoration of heroes pervaded ancient Greek civilization. This was the function of the Homeric sagas, which from the eighth century onwards sang the deeds of Achilles, Agamemnon, Odysseus, and dozens of other warriors. Likewise, the cycle of tragedies performed each year at Athens from the 490s B.C. to the second century A.D. fulfilled the same function of elevating heroes above ordinary citizens. Whereas other civilizations celebrated founders, the Greeks commemorated heroes from every epoch. When Italian humanists of the fifteenth and sixteenth centuries developed their cult of fame, they too extolled heroes for overcoming constraints of nature. Anyone who surpassed limitations imposed by nature merited undying renown.

The humanist cult of fame presupposes ambition to outdo nature, to surpass "natural" barriers by running faster, building higher, and thinking harder. As perpetuated in the cult of anniversaries, humanism honors conquest of nature rather than collaboration with it. A nineteenth-century form of competition with nature illustrates the potential for drama inherent in this approach, as mountain climbers took their place in the long roster of human accomplishment. After 1800, for example, adventurers in the Swiss Alps brought the Greek notion of duelling against nature to the task of ascending unclimbed peaks. Late nineteenth-century accounts of Alpine ascents resemble Pindaric odes that recount who "conquered" each peak first and at what cost.[8] Showing ingenuity as well as foolhardiness, men ventured where nature had not intended them to go. Rhetoric that personified nature's "intentions" reinforced belief that in order to advance, humans must defy a nature that stands opposed to them. In keeping with the Greek notion of tragedy, imprudence may, in turn, trigger nature to cause a fall. It follows that humanist anniversaries may commemorate noble failures as well as triumphs.

Since anniversaries reflect the convictions of the Greek and Italian humanists who invented them, they tend to commemorate feats of defying nature. Artists, writers, and musicians who achieved unprecedented feats of expression get commemorated because they burst the bounds of what professionals had previously deemed possible. Major creators may be likened to record-breakers in the Olympic Games; by venturing into uncharted territory, they establish new standards for others to surpass. For better or worse, the notion of artists participating in a cultural Olympics invokes the idea of progress in the arts. This notion found its classic expression in the *Lives of the Painters* (1550; 2d ed. 1568) by the painter Giorgio Vasari (1511–1574), who decreed breakthroughs by fellow Florentines like Leonardo, Michelangelo, and Raphael to be unsurpassable. Their successors, who became known as Mannerists, had no choice but to recombine elements that the masters had perfected. In formulating Mannerist strategy, which resorted to manipulating the unsurpassable by rearranging its parts, Vasari and his colleagues acknowledged that they could never outdo their models. They also anticipated a major motif of subsequent commemorations. Like today's commemorators, Mannerist artists believed that supreme achievement lay in the past and could only be aped, not surpassed or equaled. As adapted by postmoderns, the cult of anniversaries carries these assumptions one step further: what we can no longer produce we can only commemorate.

The Rise and Fall of the Avant-Garde and its Objections to the Cult of Anniversaries

By the early nineteenth century, certain artists who called themselves "modern" rebelled against academic standards of excellence and the cult of anniversaries that reinforced them. Members of the avant-garde adopted an adversary stance toward academic culture.

Feeling free to borrow from whichever previous artists they pleased, or from none at all, they no longer wished to compete against past masters on the masters' terms. Having rejected official taste, avant-garde artists dismissed commemorations like those of Schiller in 1859 or Rubens in Vienna in 1879 or Raphael in 1883 as a threat to creativity. Like certain present-day critics, they saw anniversaries as a sop to consumers rather than a spur to creators.

Innovators undertook to supplant celebrands of official culture. They dismissed commemorations as a bastion of the bourgeoisie against whom they were rebelling. Insofar as writers like Baudelaire and Flaubert or painters like Courbet and Manet rejected the academic culture of Napoleon III's Paris, they rejected the cult of commemorations that accompanied it. The avant-garde craved a new culture that would celebrate themselves rather than the old masters whom they wished to supersede. To be modern meant to repudiate the celebrands of the bourgeoisie.

As late as the 1950s, objections that the avant-garde leveled against academic culture tainted commemorations as well. Nothing has raised the status of commemorations so much as the decline and near-disappearance of the avant-garde since then.[9] Front-line artists now welcome commemorations because they no longer feel obliged to compete against celebrands from the past. Instead, today's creators collude with illustrious predecessors, whether through imitation, allusion, or parody. Every style from every period gets mimicked because no new style is being forged to supplant the old. That is the essence of postmodernism. In the arts and in scholarship, nothing now succeeds like toying with elements from the past. Everyone recombines what predecessors devised. The avant-garde has vanished, and commemorators have taken over.

Subverting the Cult of Anniversaries

If the cult of anniversaries has filled a vacuum left by the departure of the avant-garde, how can artists respond creatively to the hegemony of courtier-managers? Now that creators no longer initiate styles that might impose a profile on our time, planners face little opposition in allowing the Great Calendar to dictate priorities. After all, each year's roster exacts no lifelong commitment while preserving a niche for every taste. Of course, today's creators may still complain, as did earlier avant-gardes, that the cult of anniversaries caters to consumers of culture rather than to producers of it. However willingly intellectuals interpret each year's celebrands, they play little role in setting agendas. Where Europeans are celebrating fifty to a hundred luminaries each year, planners leave too little room for offbeat approaches. The cult of anniversaries diminishes opportunities for free-lance operators. The remainder of this book proposes ways in which today's creators can seize the initiative from courtier-managers in Europe and academics in the United States in order to pioneer novel approaches.

The challenge for innovators is to find ways either to redirect or to expand the offerings thrown up by the Great Calendar. Commemorations need to address issues other than those of national identity, civil religion, and humanist continuity. One antidote to the managers' monopoly of anniversaries involves devising what can be called counter-commemorations. Such subversive occasions would question the ways in which official planners respond to the Great Calendar. Counter-commemorators can, for example, dissent about which celebrands deserve recognition and which do not. They can suggest juxtapositions that managers have overlooked, and they can challenge the criteria of selection favored by cultural ministries. In a word, countercommemorations should aim to reshape the offerings of the Great Calendar into counterimages of official agendas.

In light of the disappearance of the avant-garde and the waning of its faith in the future, what should counterimages emphasize? At whatever cost, countercommemorators must avoid presenting themselves as a neo-avant-garde. They must acknowledge that they can no longer lead culture to new heights, but instead can at most diagnose its present condition and future prospects. Countercommemorators can shine as cultural critics, not artistic revolutionaries. Their task is to diagnose contemporary culture by adducing past examples and sketching future scenarios.

How can critics steer the cult of anniversaries toward controversial diagnoses of where culture stands and where it is heading? For better or worse, the key idea for interpreting the present state of culture is postmodernism. As applied to the arts and to scholarship, this term designates willingness to combine in witty ways approaches that once seemed mutually exclusive. Because no single style or conviction any longer holds sway, elements from all previous styles and beliefs can be combined in arresting patterns. Among its attractions, the postmodern stance promises openness, flexibility, and lack of censoriousness. It appeals to intellectuals who no longer aspire to shape the future. Among its disadvantages, it suffers from incoherence, lack of direction, and inability to forge consensus. Because it eschews passionate commitment, postmodernism means quite literally all things to all people. The cult of anniversaries has thrived in a climate that no longer imposes any standards. Into this vacuum of values has stepped the Great Calendar.

If countercommemorations are to change things, they need to exploit the openness of postmodernism in order to state principles that point beyond it. At least three obstacles impede using commemorations to counter the deficiencies of postmodernism. First, because commemorations have an ephemeral character, they do not suit proponents of coherence. Is there any way that intellectuals can exploit an ephemeral genre in order to state a case for enduring values? Second, the postmodern age craves near-exhaustive presentations of minute topics but shuns panoramas of grandiose ones. The cult of specialism resists radical explorations of values, and so do most commemorations. Third, anniversaries come up at arbitrary times without reference to planners' preferences. Is it possible to tailor deep-seated commitments to the whims of the Great Calendar?

Countercommemorators need to circumvent the three handicaps of ephemerality, specialism, and arbitrariness. The first two of these difficulties can be countered directly. Ephemerality can be overcome by repeating the same message year after year and in one venue after another. Just because commemorations are planned separately, that is no reason why a consistent point of view cannot prevail in a succession of them. Once a standpoint has been established, it can be promulgated in numerous settings. The challenge will be to disseminate not ideology but a widely shared mentality. As we shall see, the mentality that commends itself for countercommemorators during the 1990s is bimillennial consciousness. The remainder of this book will explore its potential for revolutionizing anniversaries.

Similarly, specialism can be countered simply by demonstrating the appeal of its opposite. Overviews that arrange isolated phenomena into broad contexts meet a need that specialists acknowledge whenever they venture outside their field. Panoramic commemorations address specialists beyond the confines of their specialty.[10] During the bicentennial of the French Revolution, for example, specialists in its history hesitated to adopt sweeping positions, while the public de-voured them. The success of Simon Schama's magisterial survey of France from 1778 to 1794, *Citizens* (1989), showed the hunger for panoramic interpretations. A huge audience awaits intellectuals who can fit accurate facts into convincing patterns. Countercommemora-tors need the courage to address a public of specialists in realms beyond their expertise. This is easier to do in Europe, where most commemorations unfold outside academia. Countercommemorations may find fewer partakers in American universities, where specialism reigns supreme.

Assuming that continuity and breadth can supplant ephemerality and narrowness in commemorations, how can countercommemorators deal with the handicap of arbitrariness? As we have seen, anniversa-ries can be arbitrary in a number of ways. The Great Calendar owes its influence to a randomness that favors no party and promotes no sect. But such randomness disperses any sense of common endeavor among either planners or visitors at myriad commemorations, and this very formlessness has discouraged scholars from studying commemo-rations as a whole. The most effective way to counter dispersion of focus is to emphasize connections among each year's crop of anniver-saries. Later chapters in this book propose co-commemorations that would link each year's celebrands in provocative ways. Co-commemo-rations offer a major tool for imparting significance to the promptings of the Great Calendar.

Besides randomness, commemorations suffer from other forms of arbitrariness. The chief of these is a tendency to fragmentariness caused by lack of coordination. Some commemorations are lavish, others penurious. Some target tourists, others address local residents. Some herald the universal appeal of a creator, while others exalt his home-town. Too many commemorations feature a local emphasis that thwarts comprehensiveness. To take a notable example, if one summarized the publications of the dozen or so Raphael exhibitions from 1983, they would not yield a comprehensive account of that most celebrated of painters.[11] And Raphael, together with Kafka and Luther in the same year, enjoyed the most thorough coverage of anyone in the past decade! By taking fragmentariness for granted, commemorations sub-stitute parts for the whole, drama for accuracy, and accessibility for weightiness. Commemorators tend to value vividness above defini-tiveness.

Countercommemorators can offset fragmentariness in one of two ways. They can make a virtue of it by propounding their own fragmentary interpretations to counter those of official venues. Or they can challenge the mentality that fosters fragmentariness, either by mounting an encyclopedic treatment of a particular figure, or by compiling a critique of existing commemorations. However eloquently a critique might spread dissenting views, the most effective device for achieving these goals is co-commemorations. By pairing celebrands in provocative ways, countercommemorators can slip new insights between the chinks of official doings.

Bimillennial Consciousness and the Transition beyond the Postmodern

Counter-commemorations offer a way to direct the cult of anniversaries toward more coherent and adventurous goals. Yet such measures are at best a stopgap, for they tend to multiply fragmentariness instead of supplanting it. In order to rebut criticisms of the cult of anniversaries, what is needed above all is a vision of where culture is heading. Stephen Toulmin pleads for formulating "horizons of expectation" so that what he calls "practical philosophy" can ease the transition into the Third Phase of Modernity.[12] Because the cult of anniversaries reflects the aimlessness of the postmodern era, critics need to discern what phase of culture lies over the horizon and then try to steer anniversaries toward it. The remainder of this book explores how the coming of the bimillennium in the year 2000 will affect not just the cult of anniversaries but the whole of intellectual life.

We have seen repeatedly how the cult of anniversaries reinforces dependence on the Great Calendar. After two decades of allowing the Great Calendar to set the agenda of cultural display, Europeans will be even more disposed than Americans to welcome the year 2000 as a mega-anniversary. The bimillennium will involve more, however, than an anniversary to end all anniversaries. The changeover once in a thousand years will awaken perennial anxieties and stir age-old hopes. Having a new first digit in the year cannot fail to galvanize imaginations worldwide. The electronic media will publicize the momentousness of the shift, and cultural managers everywhere will plan their agendas to exploit it. For the first time in recent memory, the electronic media, the press, and cultural managers in every country will share a common preoccupation: that of ushering out the old millennium and welcoming in the new. The concentration on a single event will exceed all bounds.

In view of the attention that the coming of the bimillennium will command, it is likely that something like bimillennial consciousness will emerge as a sequel to postmodernism. Even if bimillennial consciousness should prove short-lived or turn out to be a variant of the postmodern, its impact would be worth anticipating. But much more is at stake than that. Anniversaries during the 1990s offer clues to likely themes of bimillennial consciousness. From examining both the strengths and weaknesses of the cult of anniversaries, one can glimpse what lies over the horizon and take steps to shape it. To expand our horizons of expectation is the most exciting prospect that study of anniversaries offers.

Because anniversaries refer by definition to the past, up to now few observers have used them to chart the future. Still, signs of change are in the air. Already anniversaries incorporate a postmodern attitude that deemphasizes ideology. If this trend intensifies, official commemorations will increasingly laud inventiveness rather than group-identity. Some may even seek to elicit creativity from citizens rather than to instill identity in them. To emphasize individuality over conformity already points in the direction of bimillennial consciousness.

Postmodernism has pioneered breaking loose from past stereotypes. To some extent, anniversaries promote the breakdown of stereotypes by emphasizing thrownness as intrinsic to culture. Up to now, group-identities have been thrust upon people, or if you will *thrown* at them, rather than *chosen* by them. But in the postmodern era, when educated people can adopt countries, classes, religions, and languages almost at will, anniversaries can be used to foreshadow possible new identities. Although cultural managers prefer to use commemorations to cement existing identities, countercommemorators can use them to propose new ones. In particular, national identity can yield to both local and global identity. Instead of hallowing the old, commemorations can commend the new.

Postmodern consciousness, and even more, bimillennial consciousness, will expect commemorations not merely to confirm identities but to transcend them. Consumers who wish to expand their identity can find no richer display of alternatives than the commemorations that Europeans mount each year. Although courtier-managers design these events to consolidate citizens' sense of identity, nothing prevents visitors from drawing other lessons from them. Europe's single market of 1993 will encourage people to change language, social class, and country of domicile. Similarly, a single market in anniversaries can reshape national identities into transnational ones. That too will be a step toward bimillennial consciousness.

Besides stimulating people to grow beyond the identities into which they were born, anniversaries can act subversively in another way. European ministries of culture spend enormous sums each year celebrating men and women whose genius mocks the complacency of officialdom. Where so much attention swathes works of genius, subversive impulses are bound to erupt. To take the example of three French nineteenth-century artists who came up in 1990, it proved impossible to confine within national bounds creators of the scope of Claude Monet (1840–1926), Odilon Redon (1840–1916), and Auguste Rodin (1840–1917). The landscapes of Monet, the dreamlike images of Redon, and the writhing figures of Rodin invite reflection on transnational as well as national themes. A cult of anniversaries that has suited national managers cries out for themes larger than those of nationality.

Bimillennial consciousness will emphasize individual choice even more than postmodernism does. The new consciousness will impel each citizen to define his or her own pantheon of luminaries to set beside, or against, those whom courtier-managers deploy each year. The abundance of anniversaries ought to stimulate consumers to propose countercelebrands, as well as to propound counterimages of prevailing ones. As personal pantheons multiply, the cult of anniversaries will engender less consensus and more diversity. Just as desk-top publishing and cable television multiply consumer choices, so bimillennial consciousness will multiply the number of figures who get commemorated. As coteries of intellectuals devise commemorations to promote their own agendas, the national calendar of celebrands will compete against individual favorites. No doubt as diversity increases, Europe's nation-states will try harder than ever to promote national identity through commemorations. But when challenged by countercommemorations, official ones increasingly will have to address transnational issues.

As old and new identities proliferate, a new way of experiencing anniversaries will emerge. Bimillennial consciousness will encourage people to combine the identities they inherit with new ones of their own choosing. It will exploit commemorations as devices for diversifying identity instead of consolidating it. As the cult of anniversaries gets enlarged through the publicizing of personal pantheons, intellectuals will purvey transnational identity, thus obliging cultural managers who serve national governments to transcend national agendas. Part Two of this book offers a range of proposals for meeting all of these challenges. From traditional commemorations of national heroes to inventive pairings of subversive ones, unheralded opportunities await the cult of anniversaries. The Third Phase of Modernity promises a new phase of commemorations.

Notes

1. An excellent introduction is Michael Inwood, *Hegel: An Introduction* (New York: Oxford University Press, 1985).
2. George Weckman, "Community," *The Encyclopedia of Religion,* 3 (1987): 566–571.
3. See Rousseau, *Emile* (1762), *Confessions* (1782), and *Rêveries du promeneur solitaire* (1782). A well-reasoned reassessment is Asher Horowitz, *Rousseau, Nature, and History* (Toronto: University of Toronto Press, 1987).
4. Werner Heisenberg, "The Representation of Nature in Contemporary Physics," *Daedalus,* 87, 3 (1958): 95–108.
5. For a compact introduction by a leading anthropologist, see Edmund Leach, "Structuralism," *The Encyclopedia of Religion,* 14 (1987): 54–64.
6. Ancient spokesmen for this naturalism include Karl Marx's hero Democritus and the Roman poet Lucretius, neither of whom has ever commanded anniversary excitement.
7. For a chronicle of religious festivals in Europe since antiquity, see E.O. James, *Seasonal Feasts and Festivals* (New York: Barnes and Noble, 1961). On primitives' preference for celebrating lack of change, see John Middleton, "Theories of Magic," in *The Encyclopedia of Religion,* 9 (1987): 82–89, esp. 87–88.
8. See, for example, Leslie Stephen, *The Playground of Europe* (London: Longmans, Green, 1871).
9. On the waning of the "modernist" avant-garde in the United States, see Hilton Kramer, "Postmodern: Art and Culture in the 1980's" in *The Revenge of the Philistines: Art and Culture, 1972–1984* (New York: Free Press, 1985), pp. 1–11, esp. 2–5.
10. A bold example was an exhibition mounted in Vienna for the fiftieth

anniversary of Freud's death. It examined concepts of "the soul" in art, medicine, literature, philosophy, and psychiatry throughout the nineteenth century in every part of Europe. See Jean Clair, Cathrin Pichler, and Wolfgang Pircher, eds., *Wunderblock: Eine Geschichte der modernen Seele* (Vienna: Löcker Verlag, 1989).

11. Notable catalogs include David Alan Brown, *Raphael and America* (Washington: National Gallery of Art, 1983) and *Hommage à Raphael: Raphael et l'art français* (Paris: Réunion des musées nationaux, 1983).

12. Stephen Toulmin, *Cosmopolis: The Hidden Agenda of Modernity* (New York: Free Press, 1990), pp. 1–4.

PART TWO

Anniversaries during the 1990s and Bimillennial Consciousness

8

Anniversaries from Ancient Greece and Rome as Harbingers of the Bimillennium

Planning for the Early 1990s

Part One of this book dealt with the cult of anniversaries as a general phenomenon. Various chapters examined the appeal of anniversaries and characterized the planners who manage them. The discussion pivoted on notions like that of the Great Calendar, national and regional identity, the commemoration industry, the need of *homo rhythmicus* for recurrence, and differences between revolutionary civil religion and a courtly ethos. The prevalence of cultural anniversaries in Europe was contrasted with the predominance of founding events in the United States. Finally, it was argued that late in the 1990s, if not sooner, anniversaries will exert more influence than ever as the approach of the bimillennium energizes people to confront changes that already are sweeping the globe. If started early enough, an imaginative campaign of commemorations can help people to cope with the mixture of anxiety and hopefulness that the bimillennium will bring.

The remainder of the book discusses some of the more exciting anniversaries that lie ahead, offering novel ways to use commemorations during the 1990s. Some of the proposals dramatize unexpected juxtapositions, while others address neglected questions of cultural criticism, always with a view to raising consciousness about the bimillennium. This chapter concerns anniversaries of events from ancient Greece and Rome that come up between 1990 and 1994. Specialized though they may seem, commemorations of events from just before 1 B.C. can accustom people to do just what the bimillennium will require, namely to think in two-thousand-year spans of time. In proposing exercises for thinking across millennia, this chapter affirms that anniversaries are too important to schedule on a case-by-case basis. Part Two undertakes to plan them in a more sweeping manner.

The Authority of Classical Antiquity and Its Postmodern Eclipse

All too eager to cast off authority, the postmodern age has abandoned any sense of roots in classical antiquity. Nothing distinguishes the intellectual style of the 1980s from that of, say, the 1930s so sharply as loss of devotion to the culture of ancient Greece and Rome. From the Renaissance until the 1940s the art and literature of the ancients provided a standard by which to measure cultural achievement. Opponents as well as adherents of classicism acknowledged common roots in Greek and Roman antiquity.[1] Even the avant-gardes of the nineteenth and early twentieth centuries who overthrew a classical canon recognized its claims. Starting in the 1950s, however, and culminating in the 1980s, creators, critics, and consumers alike have jettisoned any anchor in antiquity.

Lack of veneration for antiquity is one of the traits of postmodern mentality. Indeed, the concept of "postmodern" was introduced to designate architecture that toys with classical motifs in a spirit of play rather than of deference. As defined by Charles Jencks, postmodern architecture emerged in the mid-1970s when architects began to employ classical motifs in a playful manner that denied them special status.[2] Postmodern architects invoke classical elements in witty and sometimes mocking ways in order to remind beholders that people no longer feel bound by classical standards. The classical canon that once commanded both obedience and dissent now competes as one among many options. Not since the fourteenth century has it labored under such a handicap.

In universities, disciplines in the humanities and social sciences have undergone similar liberation as the grip of positivism has yielded to a plurality of methods. The equivalent of postmodernism in academic life is what Charles Jencks calls "post-positivism." The obligation imposed by positivism to gather facts and test hypotheses on the basis of shared assumptions has given way to a smorgasbord of methodologies. Humanists have jettisoned any consensus as to what to study or how to interpret it. Postmodern academia has discarded the very idea of authority. Although critics assume that never again will intellectual life produce creators on a par with the giants of the past, hardly anyone appears to regret the loss. Amid such permissiveness the cult of anniversaries has blossomed as a way of manipulating the past for our delectation. We commemorate what we no longer desire to emulate.

In the field of Greek and Roman literature, authors who for centuries commanded reverence as unsurpassable masters now get invoked, if at all, chiefly as curiosities. The Greek inventors of genres as basic as tragedy (Aeschylus, Sophocles, and Euripides) or lyric poetry (Alcaeus, Alcman, and Sappho) or philosophy (the pre-Socratics, Socrates, Plato, and Aristotle) no longer rivet attention as the originators of discourse. Indeed, some scholars adopt an adversarial stance that accuses the Greeks of having pursued a "war culture" that excluded women, slaves, and foreigners. Far from being exemplars of virtue or truth-seeking, the ancient Athenians have been portrayed as imperialist misogynists who twisted rhetoric in order to justify enslaving their enemies.[3] Their Roman successors such as the epic poet Virgil, the lyric poet Horace, and the orator Cicero no longer get taught in secondary schools as they did in every European country until the 1950s. Unbelievable as it now seems, as late as the 1930s the ability to read Virgil and Cicero in Latin was a prerequisite for admission to college in the United States. Needless to say, academic departments of classics soldier on, their members consoled by lavish endowments that accumulated over hundreds of years. But however well financed, classical studies elicit neither respect nor affection from the public at large. Their hegemony is finished.

The one country of Western Europe where ancient culture retains some of its former esteem is Italy. This is because Italians still regard ancient Rome as a fount of national and regional identity. Sixty to seventy years ago, Mussolini urged Italians to identify with their classical forbears, and his regime did much to promote archaeology of both Etruscan and Roman sites. Fascist architecture, with its heavy masonry, outsized proportions, and interminable arches parodied ancient models, and the symbol of bundled sticks known as fasces, which ancient lictors once carried, admonished Italians to show strength through unity such as the ancients had exemplified. In heavy-handed but effective fashion, the ancestor-worship of Italy's Fascists smoothed the way for today's cult of anniversaries.

More recently the Republic of Italy has mobilized anniversaries in order to cement Italians' identification with ancient founders. In 1981 Italy celebrated the 2000th anniversary of the death of Virgil (70 B.C.– 19 B.C.). As is characteristic of Italy, the city of Mantua, located near the poet's supposed birthplace in Lombardy, took charge, making it more a Mantuan than a national affair.[4] Successful though it was, the Virgilian bimillennium illustrated a difficulty inherent in scheduling anniversaries from before the Christian era. Virgil died in 19 B.C., but because no year fell between 1 B.C. and A.D. 1, the 2000th year after his death occurred not in 1981 but in 1982. Thus all anniversaries of events from before the year A.D. 1 occur one year later than one would infer from adding the B.C. and A.D. dates. But to compound the confusion, the Mantuans, like certain other organizers, ignored this nicety. When proposing anniversaries to be held during the 1990s, this book will uphold the propriety of scheduling pre-Christian anniversaries one year later than hasty arithmetic would warrant.

A different kind of obstacle besets anniversaries from the Etruscan period. Mussolini did much to popularize the Etruscans as precursors of the Romans. Etruscan inventions like the arch, sewers, and the toga make them appeal to postmoderns as unsung innovators, but unfortunately Roman assimilation of their legacy left few dates and even fewer proper names to celebrate. Because the Romans erased Etruscan language and history, no dates remain to commemorate. Through their submersion by Rome, the Etruscans recall native peoples in Africa and the Americas whom European conquest disenfranchised two thousand years later. The Etruscans were among Western Europe's earliest victims of imperialism. In 1985 Tuscany celebrated the Year of the Etruscans, but in the nature of the case this date marked no anniversary. Given how ardently the Etruscans loved ceremonies, it seems ironic to exclude them from contemporary Europe's calendar of commemorations. Oddly, in 1989 the Etruscan Museum at the Villa Giulia in Rome omitted a chance to celebrate its own centennial. Perhaps a better way to draw the Etruscans into the cult of anniversaries would be to commemorate the publication of books that exalt them, such as George Dennis's *Cities and Cemetaries of Etruria* (1848) or D.H. Lawrence's *Etruscan Places* (1932). As these masterpieces demonstrate, Etruscan culture needs to be mourned now that it has been expropriated.

The calendar poses an additional obstacle to recognizing events that happened two thousand or more years ago. Anniversaries that command prestige involve round numbers such as two thousand or two thousand five hundred. No one wants to commemorate the 2050th or 2200th recurrence of an event, however momentous. Nor does even a high degree of symmetry guarantee a European-wide audience. The Virgilian bimillennium went largely unnoticed outside Italy, just as the bimillennium of Strasbourg in 1988 or that of Bonn in 1989 got ignored beyond its region. Now that Europeans no longer identify with ancient Greece and Rome, anniversaries honoring their heroes evoke scant interest. By itself the cult of anniversaries seems powerless to revive esteem for antiquity.

An example of a momentous anniversary that got overlooked occurred in Syracuse, Sicily, in 1988. The year marked the 2400th anniversary of the defeat of the Athenian expedition to Sicily in 413 B.C. The historian Thucydides made the downfall of the Athenian invasion at Syracuse the turning point of his *History of the Peloponnesian War*. After 413, Sparta's victory in that war became inevitable. As late as the 1950s schoolboys agonized over the starvation of Athenian prisoners in the quarries of Syracuse, and tourists still tarry there, musing on the fate of civilizations. Moreover, during the 1950s it was routine to compare the contest between the West and the Soviet Union with that between Athens and Sparta. Arnold Toynbee took the lead in formulating such parallels. But by the 1980s no one outside of Syracuse wanted to remember one of the turning points of Greek, and indeed of European, history. In 1988 the 400th anniversary of the Spanish Armada and the 200th of the eve of the French Revolution bulked far larger than the 2400th of the demise of Athenian hegemony. The failure of the Italian government and of other Europeans to notice the Thucydidean anniversary shows how far Europe has evolved from identifying with ancient fortunes. If the defeat of Athens could not elicit pathos, what chance have lesser events to do so?

Anniversaries from Ancient Rome during the 1990s

Events from Greek and Roman antiquity no longer buttress the national identity of Europeans or Americans. Where no public consensus exists to commemorate an event, planners lack the clout to impose one. The challenge in commemorating ancient luminaries during the 1990s will be to awaken interest in giants whom postmoderns have forgotten or even derided. As luck would have it, a number of weighty anniversaries from antiquity loom on the calendar, including two years with twin opportunities. The year 1993 will bring the 2000th anniversary of the death of both the poet Horace and his patron Maecenas, and the year 1995 will mark the 2400th of the death of the two tragedians Sophocles and Euripides.

How can these and similar anniversaries be dramatized to a public that no longer reads the ancients? A solution may lie in invoking the approach of the bimillennium. As the year 2000 nears, people will start to feel awe at the mere thought of two thousand years of history. By inducing people to ponder the elapse of two thousand years, Roman anniversaries from the decade leading up to 1 B.C. can help to prepare for the bimillennium itself. The more attention that bimillennia of Roman occasions command during the 1990s, the better people can weather the emotional ups and downs that the year 2000 will bring. Roman anniversaries offer nothing less than an apprenticeship in bimillennial consciousness. They deserve to be organized on a pan-European scale, with the rigors of the year 2000 in mind.

Anyone who travels to the city of Rome becomes aware of its status as an embodiment in stone and mortar of almost three thousand years of history. By 1995 visitors confronting the juxtaposition of ancient ruins with churches built across eighteen centuries and with secular monuments from every period would probably feel twinges of bimillennial consciousness even if several major anniversaries did not encourage it. During the 1990s the city of Rome will enjoy a series of rare opportunities to claim its role as the epitome of continuity.

The first of these will come in 1992 at the 2000th anniversary of Emperor Augustus's dedication of the Altar of Peace in 9 B.C. To celebrate the achievement of peace after more than a generation of civil war and colonial conquest, the emperor dedicated the Ara Pacis in 9 B.C. The fact that it took excavations spanning nearly five centuries to recover this monument adds romance to the story. The first fragments were excavated in the fifteenth century, others in 1859 and again in 1903, and still others in 1937 and 1938. Mussolini ordered the pieces gathered from half a dozen locations and reassembled on their present site in 1938, so that the Augustan Altar of Peace now stands nearly intact beside the Tiber. It enjoys the additional advantage of being protected by glass from corroding fumes. The story of its excavation and assembly links the last five hundred years of Italian history with antiquity. As Mussolini recognized, the Altar of Peace embodies continuity.

The city of Rome should exploit this 2000th anniversary to sponsor a world festival of peace. Such an event would reap several advantages. Because 1992 will also bring the 500th anniversary of Columbus's discovery of the Americas, no year could be more propitious for Rome to declare its venerability as a center of peace-making. The 1990s promise to be a decade of diminishing international tensions, at least in Europe, and the bimillennium of the Altar of Peace would provide an occasion to herald these changes. Such a commemoration would, moreover, counterbalance the trans-Atlantic and Hispanic focus of the Columbian year by recalling how much Europe in general, and Spain in particular, owes to the Roman Empire. Finally, emphasis on peace, needless to say, will appeal to all by crystallizing hopes for the year 2000.

The Great Calendar has decreed that the city of Rome will host an equally momentous anniversary one year later. The Festival of the Ara Pacis will prepare for the twin bimillennium in 1993 of the death of the poet Horace and of his patron, Maecenas. Horace (65 B.C.– 8 B.C.) was, after Virgil, the most honored of Roman poets. His lyrics celebrate leisured grace, refined pleasure, and contentment with human limitations. A satirist rather than a tragedian, a man who loved the tranquility of the countryside more than the bustle of the city, Horace epitomized the poet as country gentleman. Although his ideal of disciplined leisure may not suit the early 1990s, his association with the patron Maecenas does. As a result of Horace's praise, Maecenas (died 8 B.C.), who was a counsellor to Emperor Augustus, saw his name become synonymous with that of a patron of art or literature. It was he who urged Virgil to write the *Georgics*, and he figured in many of Horace's *Odes*. The French, Italian, and German languages adopted his name as the very word for patron (*mécène, mecenate, Mäzen*), and writers of the Augustan Age of English literature, led by John Dryden, Alexander Pope, and the Earl of Shaftesbury, adopted many of Horace's conceits in their praise of literary patrons.

The shared anniversary in 1993 of the deaths of the poet Horace and of his patron, Maecenas, offers Europeans an opportunity to mount a co-commemoration dedicated to the phenomenon of literary and artistic patronage. The timing is all the more apt because for the past twenty years historians of art and literature have been exploring this very topic. Following the breakthrough of the art historian Francis Haskell in the early 1960s, scholars have been unearthing the motives, resources, and obsessions of patrons in all periods of art and literature.[5] Fascinated more by social context than by substance, many scholars prefer studying patrons to studying creators, not least because patrons illuminate social history more directly than do artists. Conferences on "Maecenas and the Phenomenon of Patronage in Art and Literature" would highlight one of the central thrusts of postmodern scholarship.

The Year of Maecenas could explore, as well, the role that the cult of anniversaries now plays in promoting intellectual endeavor. In Europe the courtier-managers who plan anniversary commemorations have donned the mantle of Maecenas, particularly in motivating intellectuals. It behooves these Maecenasas to plan commemorations that will publicize their own function. In the United States, as we have seen, this function falls not to civil servants but to academics, who still hesitate to acknowledge the role they play as one another's patrons. Even if managers and academics want to conceal their role as patrons, a well-conceived Year of Maecenas could disclose their secret.

Nor is the conduct of academic patronage the only awkward reality that will surface. Since postmoderns tend to prefer patrons to creators, it is fitting that commemorations of Horace and Maecenas should elevate the patron above the poet. Nowadays when the volume of sales tends to dictate artistic and literary priorities, a Year of Maecenas should invite everyone to reflect on the imbalance now prevailing between market forces and creative initiative. Those who reach no market get no recognition. By emphasizing inequities in patronage, the bimillennium of 1993 should occasion less a celebration than a critique of existing arrangements in literature and the arts.

A similar opportunity will recur in 1995, when the Roman orator Cicero (106 B.C.–43 B.C.) will mark his 2100th birthday. Until forty years ago Cicero, no less than Virgil and Horace, was obligatory reading for educated people. His orations in defense of Rome's republic offered models of persuasion, even if his cause succumbed to that of Julius Caesar and the Emperor Augustus. In the wake of postmodernism, it would be fascinating to harness his anniversary as an occasion to reflect on the role of Roman literature in shaping European and American education from the fifteenth century down to the twentieth. Cicero's reputation as a master of persuasion makes him a plausible focus for conferences on the role of classical education in modernity. It is a topic that specialists in education and the classics can negotiate among themselves.

Of interest to a wider public is the role that rhetoric plays in human affairs. Cicero ranks as the quintessential rhetorician, who knew how to deploy every trick in order to captivate an audience. He can still teach how to popularize any topic. Indeed, his ability to pitch a message to any level remains the basic skill of public discourse. As it happens, in the forty years since classical literature went out of fashion, a new social science has evolved in the United States and Britain to explore the impact of rhetoric. Cicero's anniversary will provide an occasion for the discipline of Communication Studies to demonstrate its prowess as a tool for evaluating techniques of persuasion. The Year of Cicero will give American and British scholars of communications an opportunity to present their insights worldwide. Analyses of Cicero as the Great Communicator can lead to studies of how contemporary advertising, legal pleading, and teaching have modified the skills practiced by Cicero. It would be particularly piquant to examine advertising techniques in the light of Cicero's devices and to interpret television speeches as successors to Cicero's orations. The extent to which speech-making on television does or does not use Ciceronian devices ought to interest everyone in the postmodern age.

Because Communication Studies is an Anglo-American discipline, the Year of Cicero should focus on bringing its insights to the attention of Continental Europeans, who use anniversaries as an occasion for communicating ideas. To apply categories from America's Communication Studies to Europe's cult of anniversaries would enliven Cicero's anniversary.[6] A series of conferences on Cicero would offer both Europeans and Americans a chance to reflect on differences between their respective intellectual institutions and the ensuing conceptions of persuasiveness. Until forty years ago, Cicero belonged to the shared heritage of Europeans and Americans. His anniversary would invite postmoderns to explore how intellectual styles have diverged between the continents in the two generations since classical authors went out of fashion.

Cicero's ability to move an audience ought to remind today's intellectuals that many of them possess no such ability. As the bimillennium approaches, the ability to touch a wider public will carry ever greater importance, as the bimillennium begins to bring everyone's obsessions into view. Insofar as the cult of anniversaries (at least in Europe) tests an intellectual's rapport with a wider public, Cicero could provide a pretext for reassessing approaches to communicating ideas. In the name of Cicero, issues in communicating to wider publics could attract intellectuals from the most diverse fields. There could be no higher goal for an anniversary than to restore the art of popularization.

Anniversaries from Ancient Greece

Anniversaries from ancient Rome ought to stress how its institutions have helped for almost two thousand years to bind Europe together. The roles of Maecenas as archetypal patron and Cicero as archetypal orator illustrate the function of Roman example in shaping European institutions. Roman law lives on in the Roman Catholic Church no less than in the Napoleonic codes. What the Romans called the *res publica*, the "public thing," ought to come to the fore whenever a Roman anniversary is celebrated.

The cultural critic Hannah Arendt pointed out that ancient Rome pioneered the practice of cultural borrowing that has guided European civilization ever since. The word *culture* was introduced by the Romans to designate their practice of borrowing skills from the Greeks. As defined by none other than Cicero, the notion of *cultura animi* refers to Roman reception of earlier Greek philosophy, literature, and art.[7] Arendt suggested that Rome's greatest contribution was to teach Europeans how to borrow from more sophisticated civilizations without losing one's own identity. The Romans pioneered the notion of culture as something interchanged with other civilizations rather than as something wrested directly from nature. All subsequent borrowings from antiquity descend from this Roman conception of culture as assimilation of models created by others.

It follows that the cult of anniversaries perpetuates the Roman custom of honoring previous civilizations. The paradox of commemorating anniversaries from ancient Greece is that they reach us not via modern Greeks but rather via other assimilators of Greek tradition.[8] Starting with the ancient Romans, Greek inventions have fed the *cultura animi* of subsequent peoples. Indeed, European civilization, and not least the Christian religion, comprise one long process of blending Greek ideas with Jewish theology and Roman institutions. Because mainland Greece succumbed first to the Romans and then to the Turks (who were expelled only in the nineteenth century), modern Greece played hardly any role, at least until the twentieth century, in fostering its ancestors' ideals. Anniversaries from ancient Hellas involve thinkers and writers who for centuries have belonged to all of Europe.

The pervasiveness of Greek influence does not, however, guarantee sponsors for major Greek commemorations. The neglect in 1988 of the anniversary of the Athenian defeat at Syracuse illustrates the difficulty of finding organizers for ancient Greek occasions. Although educated citizens of every European country may lament the demise of Athenian hegemony, no country has incorporated that event into its national identity. Only the people of Syracuse, who live next to the quarries where the Athenian prisoners died, felt the tragedy in their bones. Perhaps not too many of them did either.

It follows that no sponsor came forward for the anniversary of a renowned Greek thinker who came up in 1990. The Sophist Protagoras (c. 481 B.C.–c. 411 B.C.) died in a shipwreck 2400 years before then. Although only a fragment of his writings remains, his saying, "Man is the measure of all things," has served since the Renaissance as a slogan for man-centered thinkers. Plato criticized the itinerant lecturer Protagoras because he preached "virtue" without probing the questions that such preaching implies. Although the anniversary of Protagoras could have been used to examine many of the same questions that Cicero might prompt in 1995, it would have been better to emphasize a different issue. Protagoras epitomizes the kind of thinker whose sayings have been systematically misunderstood. Whether exploited by allies like Marx or distorted by enemies like Plato, Protagoras is the archetypal straw man, who has seen opinions imputed to him mainly by opponents. It is, to say the least, ironic that one of the founders of Sophism has fallen prey to sophistry.

The task of commemorators of Protagoras, then, should have been to disentangle his contribution from the bramblepatch that is his reputation. Although the job of setting the record straight interests chiefly academics, such a salvage operation befits a cultural anniversary. To correct misinterpretations is all the more important in an era that holds no reputation sacred and reinterprets every text with abandon. Protagoras, who recommended making man the measure of all things, deserved a commemoration that would assess the pros and cons of reinterpretations. But because no country except Greece claimed him, he had no chance to receive his due. Hardly ever do anniversaries suffice to rehabilitate even the most deserving of forgotten thinkers.

A much weightier anniversary from ancient Greece will present itself in southern Italy in 1991. Two thousand five hundred years before that year, in 510 B.C., the Greek colony of Croton in southern Italy destroyed the neighboring colony of Sybaris. All that remains of the city of the Sybarites, who gave their name to devotees of self-indulgence, is a field of ruins on the Gulf of Taranto, while Croton survives as a thriving port. The demise of a pleasure-loving city would not deserve commemoration were it not for the fact that the rival, which defeated it, was home to one of the grandest of sages, the geometer Pythagoras. The great mathematician, whose theorem every schoolchild memorizes, taught in Croton from 531 B.C. to around 500 B.C., and it was his followers who led the city to hegemony in southern Italy. Commemorators should have no difficulty dramatizing the conflict between the asceticism of Pythagoras and the indolence of the Sybarites, because this is something that postmoderns understand only too well.

A co-commemoration of Pythagoreanism and the demise of Sybaris can be used to address many issues of the 1990s. Pythagoras is one of the towering figures of the ancient world, personifying the man of vision who saw beyond his own epoch and bequeathed wisdom in accessible form. Not only was he both sage and scientist, but he organized a community of devotees who transmitted his legacy to later generations. The obscurity that surrounds his ideas lends piquancy to the fact that he is one of the very few figures from any age whose name remains a household word. His roles as seer, scientist, and entrepreneur make him ideal for pinpointing problems of the 1990s.

Cultural critics of every persuasion can find something to praise and something to blame in Croton's defeat of Sybaris. It will be the most meaningful 2500th anniversary of the next decade. Whether one wishes to celebrate Pythagoras as a founder of European civilization or to rehabilitate the Sybarites as precursors of postmodern pleasure, a co-commemoration offers ample themes for debate. In anticipation of the bimillennium, some may wish to speculate on whether Pythagoras could have persuaded the Sybarites to work out a synthesis between asceticism and self-indulgence. For as environmentalists warn us, the need to combine asceticism with leisure pursuits will become more acute as working hours diminish and over-population undermines activities that require unlimited space. To cite just one example, the beaches of the Mediterranean, where Pythagoras once did geometry in the sand, can no longer meet the demands placed upon them. An event 2500 years ago can incite discussion of some of today's most practical concerns.

A question pertinent to all cultural anniversaries is how, if at all, the intellectual Pythagoras could have addressed the pleasure-lovers of Sybaris. The image of Pythagoras lecturing in Sybaris evokes the challenge that faces contemporary courtier-managers who seek to woo Europeans away from consumer delights to heed debates about our common future. Pythagoras was an elitist reformer whose ideas few have ever understood but whose fame endures. How can such a founder be popularized for today's Sybarites? A co-commemoration in 1991 would invite intellectuals of all camps to address this issue, which touches the very heart of the cult of anniversaries. Unpromising though it may seem, a co-commemoration of Pythagoras and the Sybarites raises questions of uncommon urgency.

Their relevance does not stop with problems of marketing debate topics to a mass market. The 2500th anniversary of the fall of one of antiquity's wealthiest cities prompts reflection on the rise and decline of civilizations. As the bimillennium approaches, anxiety about the future of civilization will mount. During the 1950s the most renowned thinker on these matters was the English historian Arnold Toynbee (1889–1975), whose centennial in 1989 could have been used to anticipate bimillennial concerns but was not (except in Japan). Toynbee's notion that a civilization emerges by meeting a challenge from its environment or its neighbors is sure to get revived as the year 2000 draws near.[9] The anniversary of Sybaris's succumbing to the challenge of Croton can bring Toynbee back onto the agenda in time to help people prepare for the bimillennium. The fact that Toynbee began his career as a historian of ancient Greece makes him a predestined mentor for the co-commemoration of 1991. He would also make a fitting commentator on the Roman Festival of the Altar of Peace in 1992.

If Toynbee were alive to assess the anniversary of 510 B.C., he might point out that Pythagoras did more than anyone else to propound a mysticism based on numbers. Indeed, there is something Pythagorean about the cult of anniversaries based on multiples of fifty and one hundred. What better time could there be to ponder the spell that these numbers cast than during the 2500th anniversary of the triumph of Pythagoras's city over that of his rivals? What could better justify Pythagoras's faith in numbers than to realize that the remains of both cities have all but disappeared (modern Crotone preserves almost none of its ancient buildings), while the cult of numbers, by which we remember them, endures? Buildings collapse but numbers abide: that is a Pythagorean theme at the heart of the cult of anniversaries .

In recognition of the mysticism of numbers, it would make sense to declare 1991 the Year of Pythagoras. This will coincide with the bicentennial of another devotee of the cult of numbers, Wolfgang Amadeus Mozart (1756–1791). It will also be the 150th anniversary of the death of the philosopher Johann Friedrich Herbart (1776–1841), whose writings popularized the philosophy of Leibniz in nineteenth-century Germany and Austria. Like Pythagoras, Herbart believed in numbers as a guide to the structure of the cosmos and would make a fitting co-celebrand, with both Mozart and Pythagoras.[10] Indeed, the Year of Pythagoras should call attention to visionaries down through the centuries who have advocated a cosmology based on numerical structure. Thinkers like the Italians Ficino, Pico, and Campanella belong with Leibniz and his successors in the roster of neo-Pythagoreans.

To assess these mystical mathematicians in one swoop will help people to think about the bimillennium in an orderly way. The neo-Pythagoreans show that a calendric shift like that of the year 2000 can instill faith in order as well as arouse fear of breakdown. The Year of Pythagoras can be used to allay anxieties about the portentousness of the bimillenium. People who realize that his thought has endured for two and a half millennia will face the transition from one millennium to the next with greater aplomb. Like the cult of anniversaries, Pythagoras, too, personifies the continuity of civilization. Until fifty years ago thinkers from antiquity presided over the great occasions of European history, facilitating adjustment to change. Pythagoras deserves to resume that role during the 1990s.

Ancient Greece will offer another anniversary in 1995, one that promises to eclipse all others from antiquity during the coming decade. Two great Athenian tragedians died in 406 B.C., the younger Euripides a few months before the elder Sophocles. Sophocles even delivered a funeral oration for his younger colleague. If imaginatively handled, the 2400th anniversary of their deaths could be one of the most stirring of prebimillennial events. Sophocles (c. 497 B.C.– 406 B.C.) and Euripides (c. 480 B.C.–406 B.C.) were two of the most original and influential writers Europe ever produced. Together with their predecessor Aeschylus (525/524 B.C.–456/455 B.C.), they rank with Dante, Shakespeare, Corneille, Racine, and Goethe as the most profound of tragic dramatists. They share the further distinction of having invented many of the devices that playwrights have used ever since, including dramatic irony, sudden reversals, the *deus ex machina*, the confidant, the messenger, and the soliloquy. The fact that both these giants died in the same year, when Athens was nearing defeat by Sparta after nearly thirty years of war, suits the cult of anniversaries to perfection. It will provide a chance to air the "adversarial mode" of classical studies as well. All countries can join in reflecting on issues of tragedy, transition, and renewal around this co-commemoration in 1995.

These two writers have, moreover, special affinity with both psychoanalysis and literary psychology. Sophocles's best-known work, *Oedipus the King* (420s) inspired Freud to coin the term *Oedipus complex.* That drama's tracking down of buried secrets anticipates psychoanalysis. Euripides, not to be outdone, pioneered the notion that Greek deities personify impulses that stir all humans. His last play, *The Bacchae,* was performed frequently during the 1960s as a warning against both puritanism and sexual license. Long after Europeans ceased to believe that the Olympian gods rule the cosmos, writers invoked them in the manner of Euripides to compose dramas about passions in conflict. Among the masters at psychologizing myths was the French tragedian Jean Racine (who had his 350th anniversary in 1989). Racinian psychology seems to anticipate equally Freudian and Jungian thought. Euripides also inspired a bevy of recent French dramatists like Jean Giraudoux, Jean Anouilh, and Jean-Paul Sartre to adapt Greek tales to twentieth-century situations. Their plays cry out to be revived during commemorations for Euripides.[11]

The very concept of tragedy has special bearing on the coming of the bimillennium. The three Greek tragedians taught subsequent Europeans to stand face-to-face with downfall, both personal and collective. To mention only a few examples, they inspired a cultural critic like Nietzsche to reflect on the Apollinian and Dionysian impulses, which in his view only tragedy can fuse.[12] They inspired the contemporary historian Thucydides to interpret the defeat of Athens by Sparta as the working out of *hubris*. It was this historian's tragic view that in turn inspired Arnold Toynbee to conceive his vision of the rise and fall of civilizations.

The notion of arrogance driven by obsession to provoke its own demise — what the Greeks called *hubris* — invites reflection on the end of an era. Sophocles and Euripides died at a time when a glorious era was ending in disaster. Their tragic view of life, which even before the downfall had taught that everyone suffers loss, interprets ruin as a punishment for human excess. Christianity in turn incorporates the tragic view by reenacting the Crucifixion every Sunday in the Eucharist. Christianity, of course, claims to have overcome the fact of death through Christ's Resurrection, and it is the promise of individual salvation that more than anything else separates Christianity from the mentality of the ancients.

The theme of loss and resurrection will preoccupy people more than ever as the bimillennium approaches. Some will adopt a tragic view, others a Christian view, and still others a comic view as the Great Changeover nears. Everyone would stand to gain by pondering plays like Sophocles's *Oedipus* Cycle (written 440–406) or Euripides's *Trojan Women* (415 B.C.) and by studying the interpretations they have received through the centuries.[13] By inculcating a long view of human affairs, Greek tragedy opens the mind to the largest issues. A revival of Sophocles and Euripides would place the coming of the bimillennium in context.

Lest tragedy lend too grave an air to preparations for the bimillennium, commemorations in 1995 can include the plays that Aristophanes wrote to satirize Euripides. The *Thesmophoriazusae* (411 B.C.) accused Euripides of defaming women, while *The Frogs* (405 B.C.) abused him for scuttling the standards of Aeschylus. To call attention to Aristophanes's preference for the old-fashioned Aeschylus over the innovator Euripides raises questions about facing cultural change at the end of an era. Athens was living through its own *fin de siècle* when Aristophanes criticized Euripides. By 1995 many people will welcome a lighthearted interlude to offset the weightiness of the bimillennium.

A co-commemoration of Sophocles and Euripides promises to bridge gaps throughout the intellectual world. It will appeal equally to Europeans and Americans. The coincidence of the masters' deaths a few months apart makes one ask whether a tragic or a comic view is better suited to the bimillennium: was it amusing or tragic that the two authors died within a few months of one another? The genre of tragedy can enlist scholars of literature, psychology, communications, art history, religion, and anthropology to examine how much European culture owes to these two masters. Their influence exceeds that of the painter Raphael, who was commemorated with maximum resources during 1983, and there is no composer, not even Mozart or Beethoven, who can rival them in impact. Sophocles and Euripides will be the two most influential cultural figures to come up for commemoration during the 1990s. To have the opportunity to celebrate both in the same year is more than any planner could have dreamed. To have this co-commemoration fall just five years before the bimillennium crowns all expectations. Then, if ever, planners will get a chance to publicize profundity.

If bimillennial consciousness has not emerged full-blown by 1995, celebrations of Sophocles and Euripides should bring it to the fore. Their prestige offers a worthy climax to the year of Pythagoras in 1991, the Peace Festival of 1992, and the year of Maecenas in 1993. Since the Year of the Tragedians will coincide with that of Cicero, the latter's focus on Communication Studies can be applied to Greek tragedy as well. How can modern resources be used to disseminate the tragic view? It is a question suitable to connect both Cicero and the tragedians with the coming of the bimillennium. Such an opportunity to popularize the weightiest matters will not come soon again.

Since the fading of classical studies forty years ago, the heritage of antiquity remains alive from day to day chiefly through its incorporation into Christianity. As if enough portentous occasions were not already looming, the year 1993 will bring the 1500th anniversary of a major transition between antiquity and Christianity. In A.D. 493 the Arian Christian Theodoric captured the city of Ravenna, which was then the capital of the Roman Empire in the West. The conqueror made Ravenna the capital of his Ostrogoth kingdom and began building churches, which still stand. They recall a time when Christians remained too mindful of persecution to adorn the exterior of a building, for unlike later church architects, Theodoric's put all the pomp on the inside.

The 1500th anniversary of the kingship of Theodoric offers Toynbeean themes aplenty. The Ostrogoths' christianizing of Roman motifs can be celebrated two years after commemorating the fall of Sybaris at the hands of Pythagoras's Croton. Theodoric's aspiration to reign as successor to the emperors exemplifies northern Europe's assimilation of Southern European traditions. The triumph of the Ostrogoth king represented the passing of an era and, as such, will suit the bimillennial mood. To celebrate a Christian patron of art in the same year as the pagan patron Maecenas will add zest to the occasion. It was through Christians like Theodoric that antiquity got handed down to us. Their accomplishment cannot help making the farsighted ask, "Who will transmit the achievements of the twentieth century beyond the year 2100?" It is a question that no one can face with equanimity. But by commemorating anniversaries from antiquity, people can begin to face the awesomeness of what is at stake.

Notes

1. Patrick Brantlinger, B*read and Circuses: Theories of Mass Culture as Social Decay* (Ithaca: Cornell University Press, 1983), expounds the use of classical antiquity as a standard by which to judge modernity.
2. Charles Jencks, *Post-Modernism: The New Classicism in Art and Architecture* (New York: Rizzoli, 1987).
3. W.R. Connor, "After Smashing the Wedgwood," *The American Scholar*, 58 (1989): 533–541, expounds these views and then defends the ancient Greeks as posers of "life and death" questions. Similar confidence pervades Alan H. Sommerstein, "Learning from the Greeks: On Human Nature, War, and Intellectual Inquiry," *Encounter*, 74 (January 1990): 12–18.
4. The Istituto della Enciclopedia Italiana published a massive *Enciclopedia Virgiliana*, 5 vols. (Rome, 1984) to mark the occasion.
5. Francis Haskell, *Patrons and Painters: A Study in the Relations between Italian Art and Society in the Age of the Baroque* (New York: Knopf, 1963).
6. A far-sighted introduction to Communication Studies is W. Barnett Pearce, *Communication and the Human Condition* (Carbondale: Southern Illinois University Press, 1989).
7. Hannah Arendt, "The Crisis in Culture: Its Social and Its Political Sig-

nificance," in *Between Past and Future: Eight Exercises in Political Thought* (New York: Viking, 1969), pp. 212–213.

8. See G.W. Clarke, ed., *Rediscovering Hellenism: The Hellenic Inheritance and the English Imagination* (Cambridge: Cambridge University Press, 1989), for ten articles reassessing English borrowings from ancient Greece, 1750 to 1850.

9. Arnold Toynbee, *A Study of History*, 12 vols. (Oxford: Oxford University Press, 1934–1961), compares twenty-one civilizations, of which seven survive. William H. McNeill, *Arnold J. Toynbee: A Life* (New York: Oxford University Press, 1989), places him in context. A negative assessment is Elie Kedourie, "Arnold Toynbee and his 'Nonsense Book'," *The New Criterion*, 8 (March 1990): 18–31.

10. On Herbart's application of mathematics to psychology, see Marianne Kubaczek, "Zend-Avesta oder das lebendige Wort," in Jean Clair, Cathrin Pichler, and Wolfgang Pircher, eds., *Wunderblock: Eine Geschichte der modernen Seele* (Vienna: Löcker Verlag, 1989), pp. 379–386.

11. Likely revivals include Giraudoux's *The Trojan War Will Not Take Place* (1935), Anouilh's *Antigone* (1943), and Sartre's *The Flies* (1943).

12. Friedrich Nietzsche, *Die Geburt der Tragödie aus dem Geiste der Musik* (Leipzig: Fritzsch, 1872), translated as *The Birth of Tragedy* (New York: Vintage Books, 1967).

13. George Steiner, *Antigones* (New York: Oxford University Press, 1984), recounts interpretations of Sophocles's play down to the present.

9

Christian Anniversaries in a Secular Age

Dilemmas of Christian Anniversaries as Illustrated by the Nazarene Painters

In our age of anniversaries, the ones with which it all began, namely Christian ones, face special obstacles. Having forgotten how much the notion of anniversaries owes to that of saints' days, secular planners seized the cult of anniversaries for themselves. Because public anniversaries have become secular occasions, Christians must lean over backwards if they are to commemorate their seminal figures without secularizing them. The preempting of the cult of anniversaries by secularists exemplifies the prevalence of non-Christian assumptions today, particularly in Europe. This chapter examines some of the difficulties confronting attempts to adapt the cult of anniversaries to Christian figures.

The Christian religion thrives by remembering certain key figures, not just Jesus, but many others, including his disciples, the evangelists, Saint Paul, the Virgin Mary, and other important saints. It is a commemorative religion, whose central act of worship, the Eucharist, is held by Catholics to reenact, and by Protestants to recall, an actual occurrence. To remember is the Christian act *par excellence*. In a sense, churchgoers need no extraliturgical commemorations since every Sunday they stage a liturgical one. Nonetheless, from the time of their origins, Christians have set aside days for venerating particular saints. Moreover, much of medieval art depicts saints in ways that can only be called commemorative. Renaissance painting continued the tradition of commemorating Christian saints, not least through depicting events from the Gospels and from the Old Testament. Catholics still commemorate saints annually on their feast day, and in Italy and Spain entire towns may join in celebrating a municipal patron.[1]

It is well known that the Council of Trent in the mid-sixteenth century encouraged Catholic parishes to display images of saints. From about 1550 to about 1750, Counter-Reformation painting flourished in Italy, France, and to a lesser extent in Germany and Austria, applying the devices of secular painting to dramatize images of saints' lives. A new attitude toward Christian art emerged in the early nineteenth century, when the young Germans who called themselves Nazarenes objected to biblical scenes that ape secular historical painting. The Nazarene painters, four of whom have anniversaries between 1988 and 1994, exemplify problems that still afflict Christian anniversaries in a secular world. These German zealots endeavored to create a style of painting that would restore to Christian art the spirit of its origins. Their failure to create an enduring style illustrates dilemmas that persist today. Problems they faced in their art recur when anyone tries to commemorate Christian occasions.

The Nazarenes were young Germans, born from 1788 on, who came to Rome in 1809 (or soon thereafter) and devoted themselves to portraying biblical scenes in a style modelled on that of the Renaissance masters Perugino and Raphael.[2] In contrast to the English Pre-Raphaelites who emerged forty years later, the Nazarenes were outspoken Raphaelites. They despised secular historical painting, which two of their founders, Franz Pforr (1788–1812) and Johann Friedrich Overbeck (1789–1869), had studied at the Vienna Academy of Art. In July 1809 in Vienna these twenty-year-olds founded what they called the St. Lukas brotherhood in honor of Saint Luke, proverbially the first painter of the Virgin. Within a few months they moved to Rome, where they settled in an abandoned Franciscan monastery, San Isidoro, on the Pincian hill. It is symbolic of their achievement that this cloister on the Via Ludovisi had been built two hundred years before to house refugee Irish Franciscans and that much of it was later demolished. Three other painters, whose anniversaries are also coming up, joined the Lukas brotherhood later. Ferdinand Olivier (1785–1841) joined the group in Vienna and painted in its spirit, although he never visited Italy. His brother Friedrich Olivier (1791–1859) followed a similar path. A major contributor, Julius Schnorr von Carolsfeld (1794–1872), met Ferdinand Olivier in Vienna and then traveled to

Rome, where he joined the brotherhood in 1818. From 1827 to 1867 he labored decorating the Residenz in Munich, while also working in Dresden.

How ought Christians to commemorate the anniversaries of the Nazarene painters? It would be easy to mount an exhibition of their frescoes, paintings, and drawings, either in Munich or in Rome. They are the archetypal religious painters of the early nineteenth century. Painters in France and England who one or two generations later tried to infuse Christian faith into painting, produced work that in its linearity and monumentality resembles that of the Nazarenes. Victor Orsel and Louis Janmot in Lyons during the 1830s and 1840s, as well as the Pre-Raphaelites in London during the 1850s, painted in a similar style. All these artists borrowed from the Italians of the fifteenth century, all produced work that looks derivative, and none of them except perhaps Janmot excelled at depicting the human figure in motion.[3] There is something frozen about the human beings drawn by the Nazarenes, as if they were suspended in another life. Instead of moving freely in pictorial space, their saints stand stiffly wearing fifteenth-century dress that is supposed to recall that of the first century. Nazarene images seem commemorative to a fault.

In their stiffness and aloofness, Nazarene paintings epitomize problems that still beset efforts to commemorate Christian occasions. Those young Germans protested against the use in religious painting of secular styles. They wanted a style that would evoke the purity, self-sacrifice, and high-mindedness that they imputed to the earliest followers of Jesus. But the style they chose evoked, instead, another period of European history, namely fifteenth-century Italy. Unfortunately, what smacked of moral purity in 1815 smacks to us of artistic impurity. When we look at Nazarene works, we see pastiches of Perugino and Raphael, and too often we see Sunday-school illustrations rather than probings of the Gospel. Because Nazarene style is derivative, not even excellent workmanship can save it from conveying the message that Christianity is second-hand.

That is the dilemma posed to planners of Christian commemorations: to use secular styles makes an occasion seem unspiritual, but so-called spiritual styles tend to go stale. A secularizer like André Malraux may have hailed the desacralization of religious art, but practicing Christians feel impelled to combat it.[4] Because the Nazarenes linked the breakthroughs of the Christian message to the breakthroughs of Raphael, the artists ended by commemorating Raphael as much as they did Jesus. Contrary to their intentions, a style they chose to foster remembrance of Jesus now elicits commemoration mainly of itself.

Any attempt to commemorate the Nazarenes in the early 1990s can only contrast with the worldwide celebrations of Raphael in 1983. Raphael offered an ideal topic for an anniversary because artists of so many generations had adapted his style to other purposes. The Nazarenes got incorporated into that year's exhibitions as one of many coteries in a long line of imitators of Raphael. If in 1983 it was easy to specify what the Nazarenes owed to Raphael and to his master, Perugino, in the early 1990s it will be difficult to highlight what they owe to the Gospel. If one regards the Nazarenes not just as artists but as believing Christians, one can anticipate that what will get commemorated is their art rather than their faith. The same holds true of saints whom artists have depicted. What gets celebrated is their image rather than their spirit. Because Christianity purports to bring spirit to life, spirituality gets thwarted whenever images and not spirit predominate.

The contradiction between spirit and images troubles Protestants more than it does Catholics. In the mid-sixteenth century the Council of Trent authorized images of the Gospel to be displayed in churches, and Catholic painting of Christian scenes flowered for another two centuries. As it happens, many of the Nazarenes were Protestants who eventually converted to Catholicism; they brought to image-making a Protestant zeal about purity of spirit. In a similar vein, the religious painters of Lyons came from a city that cultivated ascetic spirituality, and the English Pre-Raphaelites emerged within the Anglican church under the influence of Dante Gabriel Rossetti, who by descent was three-quarters Italian. When Protestant zeal for the spirit meets Catholic devotion to images, tension between spirit and form crystallizes. It is a tension that commemorators of Christian occasions still have not resolved. The rest of this chapter proposes concrete ways of doing so.

Christian Anniversaries in 1990

The cult of anniversaries emerged, as we have seen, under secular auspices, abetted by anticlericals of the French Revolution and later by Biedermeier advocates of Germany's unification. To this day the cult of anniversaries purports to substitute the claims of national identity for those of the church. Increasingly, the commemoration industry reaps the economic benefits of anniversaries, without fussing about their "message." Since the end of World War II, the cult of anniversaries has helped secular national culture and its economic infrastructure to eclipse Christian culture, particularly in Europe. Although anniversaries owe their origin to Christian devotion to the saints, they have become secularized into a tool of the state and a device for promoting tourism.

How can Christians exploit a secular contrivance in order to celebrate their own mentors? This question prompts many further ones. Insofar as the cult of anniversaries serves secular ends, what can Christians hope to gain by turning it to their own purposes? Will not commemorations of Christian figures mirror secular practices? This prospect inevitably evokes Protestant dread of substituting images for spirit. At a more practical level, since nation-states use anniversaries to promote national and regional identity, how can Christians use the same devices to promote Christian identity? All these questions boil down to just one: What sort of compromise is possible between secular publicity-seeking and religious devotion?

The three most successful Christian commemorations of the 1980s came early in the decade, before the cult of anniversaries had run riot. They included Saint Benedict's 1500th anniversary in 1980, Saint Francis's 800th in 1982, and Martin Luther's 500th in 1983. All three recalled the birth of founders who had shaped secular as well as religious institutions. Saint Benedict commended himself to humanists because his order's monasteries had transmitted manuscripts from late antiquity down to the Renaissance. Although the Benedictine year was observed all over Europe, it appealed above all to scholars, not a few of whom construed the saint as a servant more of humanism than of God.[5]

Like Saint Benedict, whose own order undertook to commemorate him, Saint Francis could count on Franciscans to dramatize his 800th anniversary. Franciscan churches installed photo displays, featured exhibitions of Saint Francis in art, and sponsored pilgrimages not only to Assisi but to other haunts like La Verna. Because the year of Saint Francis proved more devotional and less humanist than the Benedictine one, it is probable that many secularists scarcely noticed it. It was above all an affair of the faithful.

The same cannot be said of the Luther year in 1983, which offered a pretext for national image-building in both East and West Germany. East Germany sponsored conferences at Luther's haunts in Wittenberg and elsewhere, while West German historians explored Luther's impact on every aspect of German culture.[6] Because Luther had commanded Christians to obey the state under all circumstances, it was easy for cultural ministries to preempt him. It seems all the more ironic, therefore, that Luther celebrations in East Germany fortified the Lutheran church, which did so much in the following years to buttress opposition to the regime. In both East and West, the Luther year encouraged expressions of German national identity. Among Christians it promoted dialogue between Catholics and Protestants, during which both parties realized how many Lutheran practices the Second Vatican Council had adopted in the early 1960s. Because the Catholic church now stresses Bible-reading, worship in the vernacular, and commitment to ongoing reform, Catholics used the 500th anniversary to discover how much present-day Catholicism owes to Luther.

It is unlikely that any Christian anniversary of the 1990s will command a similar breadth of support. This is not because the figures to be commemorated are minor, but rather because they do not reinforce national identity the way Saint Francis does in Italy or Luther does in Germany. To be sure, two giants of the medieval church came up as early as 1990: Saint Gregory the Great marked the 1400th of the beginning of his pontificate (in 590), and Saint Bernard of Clairvaux the 900th of his birth (in 1090). If commemorations emphasized scope of achievement instead of present-day resonance, Gregory the Great would have towered over the year 1990. He ranks with Saint Benedict as one of the founders and preservers not just of the church but of European culture. No fewer than six epochal achievements fall to his credit.[7] It was Gregory who ratified Benedictine monasticism and regularized the cure of souls throughout Europe. Gregorian chant originated with him, as did medieval conceptions of a bishop's authority. He also initiated the temporal power of the Papacy and launched the conversion of Britain by Saint Augustine of Canterbury. Few if any other Europeans have established so many enduring practices as did Saint Gregory the Great.

And yet the anniversary of his pontificate passed largely unnoticed, even among Catholics. To be sure, he elicited a scholarly conference in May at the Vatican, sponsored by Augustinian canons, but the American Society of Church History devoted only one session to him at their annual conference. The media, moreover, paid scant attention, perhaps because few wished to salute a man who had inaugurated institutions like the Papal States and belief in purgatory, which Protestants, secularists, and not a few Catholics join in deploring. In a word, a founder of his stature affronts today's rejection of authority. Although Gregory the Great exerted unparalleled authority for more than a thousand years, his are accomplishments that few can applaud in the year 1990. Gregory laid the foundations for the Western church as an international body, whereas Europe's nation-states base their unity not on religion but on economics and politics. Indeed, Gregory's success in unifying Europe around Catholicism might seem to distract from the aspiration of the European Economic Community to achieve a single market by 1993. Commemorators at the Vatican Conference in May 1990 can be forgiven for protesting that the most enterprising celebrand of 1990 was unduly ignored.

Saint Bernard (1090–1153) of Clairvaux enjoyed an advantage over Saint Gregory in that a monastic order stood ready to promote his anniversary. The Cistercian order, which he led but did not found, is a stricter branch of the Benedictines, and that order organized several conferences in Paris, Cluny, and elsewhere to weigh his influence. Needless to say, the enthusiasm of scholars cannot make a monastic reformer popular. Austerities may command respect, but few will wish to imitate them. For all his saintliness, Saint Bernard seems dated, not least because of his militancy against unbelievers and against Islam. Nevertheless, he practiced and taught others to practice the kind of purity to which the Nazarene painters aspired. He personifies an otherworldliness that commemorations can only hint at.[8]

For that reason, if no other, this man of piety would have been best commemorated through a dramatic gesture, and a potential one lay ready to hand. The French state could have undertaken to redress an affront to Saint Bernard that Napoleon had enacted almost two hundred years ago. During the twelfth century the Cistercians built abbeys all over Europe. Routinely they sent an abbot and twelve monks to clear forests and plant settlements in Germany, Scandinavia, northern England, and Spain as well as throughout France. In the course of this activity, the Cistercian style of romanesque architecture spread like wildfire. How ironic it is, therefore, that the abbey of Clairvaux, which that great builder Saint Bernard founded in 1115 and which he served as abbot until his death in 1153, can no longer be visited. For in 1808

Napoleon transformed into a state prison the monastery that Saint Bernard's successors had inhabited as late as 1790.

To this day the site of Clairvaux functions as a prison. Among its most famous prisoners was a Jacobin revolutionary, Auguste Blanqui (1805–1881), who stayed there during the early 1870s. The conjunction of Saint Bernard occupying the same site as the anticlerical fanatic Blanqui is one of those oddities that only Christian history could devise. The most fitting recognition of Saint Bernard's 900th anniversary would have been for the French state to dismantle the prison at Clairvaux and restore it as a Cistercian museum (incorporating the library of the monastery now preserved at Troyes). Since, moreover, the site of Clairvaux lies just a few kilometers southwest of the home of General de Gaulle (1890–1970) at Colombey-les-Deux-Églises, it would have been doubly meaningful to execute this transfer during a year when the two men shared an anniversary. Unfortunately, coming on the heels of the bicentennial of the French Revolution, such an act of generosity by the state toward a doctor of the Church proved impossible. An anticlerical state could not allow a Christian anniversary to inspire policy, nor had the commemoration industry enough to gain by the restoration of Clairvaux.

The third figure to be commemorated during 1990 posed a different set of problems. John Henry, Cardinal Newman (1801–1890), who valued coherence above all else, personified issues that continue to divide Roman Catholics from Anglicans. Master of one of the noblest prose styles of the nineteenth century and visionary of liberal education, Newman risked having his anniversary founder because he means contradictory things to rival groups.[9] Anglicans cannot forgive the most eloquent and winsome of their leaders for having converted to Rome in 1845, while Catholics do not wish to acknowledge that Anglicanism bred one of their towering thinkers.

And yet Newman deserved a comprehensive commemoration because, more than almost any other nineteenth-century churchman, he anticipated the dilemmas of Christianity in the postmodern era. His notion of authority as something that grows to fit expanding consciousness suits the 1990s. His conception of assent as a response to symbols removes the task of proof from the realm of science and transfers it to that of lived experience, where flexible criteria prevail. His marshalling of categories into hierarchies shows how parts fit into wholes, which transcend the claims of any party. So sophisticated is his technique for relating parts to wholes that it could help any institution to rethink its goals. But because Newman transcends any camp that may claim him, none can commemorate him adequately. His very stature precludes a conventional approach.

Cardinal Newman as "Arbiter of Commemorations" during 1990

If Cardinal Newman were to receive the kind of commemoration he deserves, planners would have needed to relate the cult of anniversaries in Europe to the revival of religion that is burgeoning everywhere else. In Africa, Asia (notably in Korea), and in Latin America, Christianity is expanding faster than ever before, while Islam attracts new followers as it acquires fresh vigor, and both Hinduism and Buddhism are undergoing renewal. Not only are new members joining established religions, but new syncretistic cults are emerging worldwide.[10] The positivists of the earlier twentieth century who forecast the demise of religion have proven mistaken everywhere except in Western Europe, the heartland of cultural commemorations.

Reasons for Western Europe's commitment to secularism abound. The traumas of two world wars and the Holocaust have not yet healed. Many Europeans have not quite absolved Christian churches of co-responsibility for the rise of Hitler and Stalin and for slackness in opposing them. Europe's need to mourn the havoc of the first half of the century accompanies a conviction that atrocities committed in the name of Nazism and Marxism sprang from distortions of Christianity. Instead of reviving the Christian faith as Americans and East Europeans are doing, West Europeans prefer to commemorate cultural figures, particularly those of earlier centuries who cannot be blamed for the catastrophes of this one. Part of the significance of the bimillennium for Europe is that the coming of the year 2000 will shift the disasters of "this" century back to a previous one. Once Europeans no longer live in the century of Hitler, Stalin, and the Holocaust, the need to apportion blame will surely diminish. The coming of democracy to Poland, East Germany, Czechoslovakia, Hungary, and Romania during 1989 has further accelerated this process of outgrowing the past.

Given that Western Europe has shunned reviving Christianity, to what extent, one may ask, does Western Europe's cult of anniversaries function as a substitute for religion? Similarities between Christianity and the cult of anniversaries run deep. Just as resort to the Great

Calendar evokes the uncontrollable in life, so Christianity teaches that humans do not control destiny. Both views call attention to the element of thrownness in life. Instead of venerating Christian saints, West Europeans are invited to venerate secular creators in accord with a timing that is inherited, not chosen. As Eviatar Zerubavel shows, humans crave a recurring rhythm within which special events can highlight certain days and years. In keeping with the needs of *homo rhythmicus*, each year's roster of anniversaries locates participants in time as well as space. Like a major religion, the cult of anniversaries commands consensus among diverse nationalities and professions, it celebrates the rhythms of birth and death, and it directs attention to the mysteries of the cosmos. Inevitably a probing commemoration will raise questions like: How did a creator achieve the breakthroughs he did? Why did this celebrand succeed where others failed? Even if these questions get answered in a secular way, they have a religious depth to them. To ponder the mysteries of creativity can meet a religious need, particularly if the occasion gratifies the need for rhythm.

The anticlericals of the French Revolution sought to substitute a civil religion for the Christian one. To judge by today's upsurge of anniversaries in Europe, they and their successors succeeded beyond their wildest dreams in establishing a religion of culture. Anniversaries provide the rituals of a civil religion that venerates European culture in all its facets. A humanist pantheon has replaced for many, if not most, Europeans the Christian communion of saints. The question for Christians who wish to participate in this process is what role should they play in a cult that tends to obscure Christian contributions?

For a start, they can invoke Christian celebrands as a lens through which to interpret secular ones of the same year. During 1990 no one commended himself so well for the role of "Arbiter of Commemorations" as Cardinal Newman. Christians and secularists alike would profit by imagining how Cardinal Newman might interact with fellow celebrands during 1990. To interpret Christian and secular figures in tandem is to overcome traditional splits, and in so doing to move toward bimillennial consciousness.

It is worth examining some of the opportunities for co-commemorations that Newman and his fellow celebrands presented. The National Portrait Gallery in London honored Newman with a comprehensive exhibition, as did the Bodleian Library in Oxford, but neither linked him with other celebrands of 1990. Although none of the following proposals got implemented, mention of them illustrates the potential for breakthroughs. Chapter Two compared Cardinal Newman and Thomas Hardy regarding their views on thrownness. Another piquant comparison involves juxtaposing the biographer James Boswell (1740–1795) with Cardinal Newman. The mere pairing of their names raises a number of questions. How would Newman look different to us if someone had recorded his utterances across twenty years as Boswell had for Johnson? More important, to what extent can Newman function for us as a sage the way Johnson did for the late eighteenth century? With men of such divergent calling, what needs to be compared is not so much their religious or ideological beliefs as the way they played their social roles. To a surprising degree, Newman is a Catholic Johnson; both men affirmed common sense, liberal education, and the authority of tradition. Ten or twenty years from now, ability to discern such parallels may well be a commonplace of bimillennial consciousness. To use co-commemorations to promote such awareness marks a first step in that direction.

Other British co-celebrands included the economist Adam Smith (1723–1790), the founder of the science of economics. Newman's conviction that liberal education entails reading texts of every discipline and all persuasions makes it plausible to inquire how an economist and a theologian consort together. Smith's role as a moralist can be compared to that of Newman, and the economist's involvement in his native Scotland raises the question of what significance Newman can have for Presbyterians. Although the leading economists who convened in Edinburgh during July 1990 to honor Adam Smith scarcely mentioned Cardinal Newman, these two personify the kind of improbable coupling that bimillennial consciousness will savor.

Openness to improbable pairings gets more severely tested when Newman is aligned with his near contemporary, Beau Brummell (1778–1840). The fashionplate of English dandies, who died in isolation in Caen, seems utterly remote from the eloquent churchman, whether in his Anglican or his Catholic phase. Yet Brummell's pursuit of outward impeccability bears more than one connection to Newman's pursuit of an inner light. During the 1830s Newman preached at Oxford to admirers of Brummell, and both then and later more than a few dandies converted to Christianity, often to the sort of Anglo-Catholicism that the young Newman promoted. Even French dandies like the Norman writer Jules-Amédée Barbey-d'Aurevilly (1808–1889) favored Catholicism. Such unexpected affinities are what bimillennial co-commemorations should bring to light. "Opposites attract" might be the motto of Newman's tenure as "Arbiter of Commemorations." He of all people would have savored improbable alignments, and as an educator he would have insisted on publicizing them. A man who strove as hard as Newman did to shatter barriers would have rejoiced at the spread of bimillennial consciousness.

Several other English co-celebrands fit more naturally than any of the above into Newman's vision. Robert Burton (1577–1640), who once served as a vicar in Oxford, wrote a book that foreshadows Newman's all-encompassing humanity. Burton's *The Anatomy of Melancholy* (1621) demonstrates rhetorical flair, Christian humanism, and a wry sense of humor that anticipate similar gifts in Newman. A conference on Burton and Newman as master stylists and interpreters of human foibles could have placed both in a brighter light. As it is, the two received successive exhibitions at the Bodleian Library, Oxford, but how many visitors tried to compare them? Another obvious co-commemoration would have aligned Newman with his Anglican contemporary, the composer Sir John Stainer (1840–1901). Stainer's setting of *The Crucifixion* (1887) would make a splendid choice to play at memorial services for Newman. No less apt would be Sir Edward Elgar's 1900 oratorio setting of Newman's poem *The Dream of Gerontius* (1866). To perform an oratorio in honor of Newman would be particularly fitting because he served the Oratorian order, in one of whose chapels in Rome that genre of music originated. An ideal setting for *The Dream of Gerontius* would be the room known as the Oratorio attached to the Nuova Chiesa, the very room which in 1600 gave its name to a new form of sacred music. Newman the Oratorian must have delighted in the coincidence.

It requires somewhat more ingenuity to pair Cardinal Newman with the French celebrands of 1990. To do so would have been all the more worthwhile because although Newman is a figure of universal scope, his appeal has yet to dawn on the Continent. The anticlericalism that still pervades France obstructs allowing a cardinal to receive co-commemorations with his contemporaries. As soon as Newman gets juxtaposed with writers like Alphonse de Lamartine (1790–1861) or Emile Zola (1840–1902), his national bent becomes all too obvious. On the surface at least, the English churchman has more in common with an opponent of the French Revolution like the Vicomte de Bonald (1754–1840). The latter's conception of tradition as a body of doctrine that preserves decrees stemming directly from God differs from Newman's notion of tradition as a body of thought that continues to evolve. A conference on Bonald and Newman could have compared these ideas to those of a book that marked its 200th anniversary, Edmund Burke's *Reflections on the Revolution in France* (1790). Burke's notion of tradition as a social contract linking the living, the dead, and the unborn anticipates Newman's concept and contrasts with that of French conservatives. France's lack of theorists who conceive of tradition as perpetually evolving has made French conservatism unduly rigid. Newman is just the thinker to correct that deficiency.

To emphasize the point, both Burke's *Reflections* and Newman's *Essay on the Development of Christian Doctrine* (1845) deserved to be yoked to another major anniversary of 1990, that of the French statesman General Charles de Gaulle (1890–1970). For all his antipathy to English insularity, the founder of France's Fifth Republic brought to statesmanship an English awareness that tradition must adapt to changing circumstances. To explore analogies between Newman's notion of change in theology and de Gaulle's implementation of change in French politics would have yielded unexpected dividends. By imparting a British flavor to commemorations of Gaullism, it would have anticipated the ferment appropriate to the bimillennium. Even Mrs. Thatcher, who is no Francophile, might have found food for thought in comparing Cardinal Newman with General de Gaulle.

Cardinal Newman himself stated principles that illuminate such endeavors. In *The Idea of a University Defined* (3d ed. 1873), Newman argued that in a university all philosophical and cultural positions should stand forth. Far from wishing to constrict the scope of Christian education, Newman strove to enlarge it. His insistence that students and professors alike weigh the widest range of options gives him a postmodern ring. His conviction that traditions of thought cannot help evolving suits the role that the cult of anniversaries plays in bringing celebrands up-to-date. In urging the educated to tackle luminaries of religious and secular bent alike, Newman made universal thinkers seem more universal, and sectarian ones more limited.

The cult of anniversaries cries out for new energy to animate it. Instead of merely rehearsing what celebrands achieved, commemorators should juxtapose provocative partners in the hope of kindling fresh insight. In particular, pairings between Christian and secular thinkers can pioneer a new attitude. Insofar as secular anniversaries have become a substitute religion, celebrands who furthered both secular and religious culture deserve special mention. Since they are few in number, a still better tactic would be to link religious advocates with secular ones. Co-commemorations can splice together what previous generations kept apart.

By examining religious figures who appeal to the educated, this chapter has sought to counteract the cult of specialism that marks the twentieth century. The challenge for Christians is to insert their heroes alongside those of the secular planners who control national and regional agendas. The goal is not to provoke controversy between Christians and secularists so much as to show that the bimillennium calls for a new attitude. Old battlelines will fade as new aspirations dawn. The time has come to move away from the militancy of Gregory the Great and Saint Bernard on the one side and Voltaire and Freud on the other. Since no past thinker fully personifies reconciliation of Christian and secular wisdom, one way to foreshadow it is to pair Christian and secular thinkers in co-commemorations. If the cult of anniversaries serves no other purpose than that of reconciling previously warring camps, it will have justified its existence.

Notes

1. It was characteristic of older piety that Alban Butler organized his *Lives of the Saints* (first published 1756–1759) by days of the calendar. See Donald Attwater, ed., *The Lives of the Saints*, rev. ed., 5 vols. (Westminster, Md.: Christian Classics, 1956). For an account of older religious festivals in Britain, also organized by the calendar, see Dorothy Gladys Spicer, *Yearbook of English Festivals* (New York: Wilson, 1954).
2. Keith Andrews, *The Nazarenes: A Brotherhood of German Painters in Rome* (Oxford: Clarendon Press, 1964); William Vaughan, *German Romantic Painting* (New Haven: Yale University Press, 1980), pp. 163–190.
3. Elisabeth Hardouin-Fugier, *Le Poème de l'âme par Janmot: Étude iconologique* (Lyon: Presses Universitaires de Lyon, 1977).
4. André Malraux, *La Métamorphose des dieux* (Paris: Gallimard 1957), translated as *The Metamorphosis of the Gods* (Garden City: Doubleday, 1960).
5. A monument of the year was Dom Pieter Batselier, O.S.B., ed., *Saint*

Benedict: Father of Western Civilization (New York: Alpine Fine Arts Collection, 1981); translated from the Belgian edition.

6. Werner Hofmann, *Luther und die Folgen für die Kunst* (Munich: Prestel, 1983).

7. Carole Straw, *Gregory the Great: Perfection in Imperfection* (Berkeley: University of California Press, 1988).

8. A compact introduction is G.R. Evans, *The Mind of St. Bernard of Clairvaux* (Oxford: Clarendon Press, 1983). In 1977 a bevy of publications marked the 800th anniversary of St. Bernard's canonization.

9. An excellent brief introduction is Owen Chadwick, *Newman* (Oxford: Oxford University Press, 1983). On Newman as educator, see A. Dwight Culler, *The Imperial Intellect: A Study of Newman's Educational Ideal* (New Haven: Yale University Press, 1955).

10. Harvey Cox, *Many Mansions: A Christian's Encounter with Other Faiths* (Boston: Beacon Press, 1988), explores this revival around the globe. He offers no explanation for its absence in Europe. On syncretistic cults, see Ninian Smart, *The Religious Experience of Mankind*, 3d ed. (New York: Charles Scribner's Sons, 1984), esp. pp. 69–71, 585, and Bennetta Jules-Rosette, "African Religions: Modern Movements," *The Encyclopedia of Religion*, 1 (1987): 82–89.

10

Beyond Postmodernism: From the Age of Anniversaries to Bimillennial Consciousness

Escape from the Past via the Cult of Anniversaries

Has the cult of anniversaries overshot itself? Perhaps the simplest explanation for recent obsession with anniversaries is the best: The public in Europe and the United States has so lost contact with the past that only extravaganzas can recall it. Is it possible that obsession with anniversaries indicates not a recovery of interest in the past but rather a loss of it? The upsurge of anniversaries in the late twentieth-century may show that postmoderns have jettisoned the past except as an occasion for mounting commemorations. Anniversaries have to be administered because too few people would heed them otherwise.

Instead of indicating commitment to the past, the cult of anniversaries expresses withdrawal from it. People commemorate what they can no longer venerate. In an age that values the present above all, anniversaries elevate certain events into guideposts across the centuries. Anniversaries enliven the present for *homo rhythmicus* by particularizing each year within the cycle of centuries. The calendar of anniversaries helps cultural managers to schedule "bread and circuses" around easily recognized themes, while the commemoration industry aims not so much to revere achievements from the past as to enhance economic growth in the present. The bicentennial of the French Revolution and the quincentenary of Columbus's first voyage provide jobs and media focus while encouraging intellectuals to talk about the relevance of preselected years to the here and now.

To interpret anniversaries as an expression of present-mindedness accords with the emergence of the heritage industry throughout Europe and North America. The heritage industry preserves sites from the past in more or less accurate replicas so that tourists can linger in a nineteenth-century factory town or an Anglo-Saxon village or a frontier fort. Although the building materials usually mirror the twentieth century, visitors welcome any resemblance, however arbitrary, to past styles of architecture and costume. The heritage industry has developed furthest in Britain, which has built dozens of "living museums," some of them, like the "London of 1588" at Tilbury Fort in 1988, lasting just for a season.[1] However ardently tourists in England care about tradition, they do not demand exactitude in reproducing the look of the past. The commemoration industry markets replicas and restorations as a substitute for authentic foci of memory.

Like the cult of anniversaries, the heritage industry caters to the appetite of consumer society for products that evoke the past without provoking debate about it. At best, the past elicits deference, heightened by neither veneration nor revulsion. With the notable exception of events from the Nazi regime, the cult of anniversaries entices consumers without tapping their obsessions. Postmodern insouciance has liberated contemporaries from any feeling that they must either repeat or shun a particular past. By granting to consumers a choice of heroes that the nineteenth century reserved for priests and schoolmasters, postmodern mentality allows year-long flirtations with the past to replace feelings of indebtedness to it.

Yet as the bimillennium approaches, the cult of anniversaries promises to give way to a less regimented approach. Commemorations orchestrated by managers to boost national prestige and promote tourism will remain with us, but by the late 1990s they will have to compete with events organized around the theme of the bimillennium. Because it will appeal to all nations, classes, and age-groups, the bimillennium promises to take on a life of its own, transcending the apparatus of the commemoration industry. It is thus time to explore how bimillennial consciousness will transform the cult of anniversaries.

Disadvantages of the Great Calendar as Legitimator of Agendas

By definition the concept of "postmodern" is transitional. Any stance that labels itself by reference to a predecessor smacks of planned obsolescence. This chapter explores how the cult of anniversaries offers clues to the mentality that lies over the horizon as a sequel and competitor to postmodernism. Stephen Toulmin has remarked that postmodernism tends "to back into the future" instead of facing it head on.[2] Study of how the bimillennium will affect anniversaries offers a chance to frame a "horizon of expectation" so that we can steer a clear course into what Toulmin calls the Third Phase of Modernity. The coming of the bimillennium means, among other things, that during the present decade, pondering the future will become ever more fashionable.

The Great Calendar, upon which postmoderns rely to an unprecedented degree, holds a climax in store for everyone. Insofar as the bimillennium will involve an anniversary to end all anniversaries, it will eclipse expectations that have emerged during this age of anniversaries. This chapter expands suggestions made previously about harnessing anniversaries to bimillennial consciousness. It inquires into characteristics of that consciousness and assesses commemorations of the late 1990s. The emphasis falls on the European mode of commemorating creators rather than the American one of commemorating events, because creators have more to say about the bimillennium.

By allowing anniversaries of all births and deaths every fifty years, the Great Calendar brings every notable to public scrutiny at least once in a half century, and usually more often. The impartiality of the Great Calendar corresponds to the openness of postmodernism toward all facets of creativity. Just as the Great Calendar reminds us of forgotten innovators and juxtaposes them with unlikely co-celebrands, so postmodern scholars delight in resurrecting forgotten creators and in positing previously unnoticed juxtapositions.[3] Postmodern sensibility subverts ideologies and canons by ceaselessly rearranging them.

As it happens, during the 1980s a parallel breakthrough occurred in the technology for reproducing music. During the postmodern years, musical performance underwent a revolution through the advent of the electronic synthesizer. A synthesizer places at the fingertips of its operator performances of all previous music in all possible transpositions. Any melody or harmonization played by any instrument in any key can be mixed with any other or transposed into infinite variations. One person sitting at a console can execute any of these manipulations beyond the wildest dreams of any predecessor. A virtuoso of the electronic keyboard can perform previously unheard of feats, instantly juxtaposing and blending musical examples the way post-modern critics do with literature, architecture, and everything else.

The Great Calendar can be likened to a synthesizer, which out of the repertoire of the past throws up the most unlikely combinations. The Great Calendar is a cultural synthesizer, which invites its devotees to combine cultural figures and themes with unheard of ease. The notion of co-commemorations can do for cultural programming what an electronic synthesizer does for music: it shatters fixations by facilitating new combinations. The Great Calendar enables anyone to reshuffle the entire patrimony in just the way that a synthesizer enables one to rearrange music. Both invite radical breakthroughs.

Just as the resources of a synthesizer outdo what musicians sitting together can perform, so virtuosos of the Great Calendar can combine figures and ideas that never met before. Although the Great Calendar has always existed, Western culture had to wait for postmoderns to tap its potential as a device for focusing priorities and undercutting ideologies. To date, it has served above all to provide managers, performers, and audiences a bastion of consensus amid a sea of options. The commemoration industry thrives on the reliability of the Great Calendar.

Up to now few managers have grasped the potential of the Great Calendar for initiating novel approaches. To take an example from 1989, the conjunction of the French Revolutionary bicentennial with both the 150th anniversary of photography and the 100th of the color theorist Michel-Eugène Chevreul (1786–1889) threw up myriad possibilities that never got tapped. Let us now mix some of those options as an electronic synthesizer might do. By conjoining photography with the Revolution, for example, one can imagine how the events of 1789 might have looked through the lens of a camera. The seven-hour film *The Revolution*, which premiered in the fall of 1989, did just that. If we reverse the comparison, we can see that starting in 1839, the camera itself launched several revolutions: visual, journalistic, and social. Just as imagining the intervention of the camera dramatizes the French Revolution, so the metaphor of revolution highlights the camera's impact.

If we go on to combine the notion of a camera-eye view of the Revolution with a third anniversary, namely that of the color theorist Chevreul, possibilities multiply. His theory that the eye blends adjoining colors into recognizable images provides a metaphor for how postmodern sensibility mixes cultural phenomena.[4] Just as Chevreul explained how Impressionist painters could juxtapose colors to mix in the eye, so the Great Calendar encourages postmoderns to juxtapose events that will mix in the mind. Juxtaposing the French Revolution with other anniversaries allows us to reconfigure its events and personages into patterns that blend like Impressionist pigments. If the camera stimulates us to rethink the Revolution through a sequence of snapshots, Chevreul authorizes us to reshuffle these into novel patterns. A historian, for example, can mix into new sequences what he imagines a camera might have captured during the 1790s. Almost effortlessly, three commemorations from 1989 yield in this way a metaphor to articulate postmodern freedom of interpretation. If applied systematically, blending of anniversaries can stimulate interpreters to redeploy images about any era whatsoever. The synthesizer of culture that is the Great Calendar stimulates us to rethink heritage from the ground up.

Cultural managers have used the Great Calendar to promote consensus about identity, whether national, regional, religious, or class-based. To date, the Great Calendar has served to generate consensus for public occasions, but its potential to renew private musing has scarcely been tapped. A parallel to the evolution of computers may be helpful to explain this difference. Use of the Great Calendar for public rather than private purposes is like use of mainframe computers before personal computers preempted the market. The Great Calendar has functioned like a mainframe computer, which cultural managers manipulate on behalf of the public. The cult of anniversaries has not yet entered the phase of the personal computer, when it will incite individuals to affirm their individuality. Moreover, just as managers' use of the Great Calendar corresponds to postmodern collapse of ideologies, so private resort to the Great Calendar may well correspond to bimillennial pursuit of idiosyncrasy. No longer will everyone commemorate the same figures at the same time, but instead those so inclined will blend favorite celebrands into unique combinations.

To date, cultural managers have used the Great Calendar to narrow rather than enlarge the range of options offered in a given year. So long as consumers let the Great Calendar dictate the timing of public celebrations, planners will continue to exploit it. Presumably, the "Stabilizer of agendas" will endure in that role until it faces a crisis. But as we know, a crisis lies just over the horizon in the year 2000. Innovators who delight in juxtaposing celebrands of a given year from different centuries or countries have not yet realized how the year 2000 will shatter even these constraints. When consumers begin to scan the two thousand years of the Christian Era, not to mention the millennia before it, they will not settle for commemorating figures born or deceased in multiples of fifty from the year 2000. Instead, everyone and everything will come up for appraisal in that year.

As soon as people begin to realize that the bimillennium encapsulates every anniversary within it, commemorations will become ever more feverish. The year 2000 will provoke syntheses not just of the years 500, 1000, 1500. and 1900, but of all previous ones. It will invite surveys of entire centuries and indeed millennia, focusing more on decades and periods than on individual years. Because of the plethora of phenomena to commemorate, the bimillennium will have to extend through the years 2000 and 2001, the former being devoted primarily to retrospectives and the latter to prospecting the future.

The bimillennium will weave together into one grand synthesis the threads of all previous Western and non-Western cultures. The year 2000 will open the floodgates of commemorative consciousness by inviting people around the world to embrace everything at once. The convention of limiting commemorations to one year's celebrands will seem arbitrary when all of human achievement comes up for review. The bimillennium will bring all cultural accomplishments into a network, applying to everything the Chevreulian notion of blending adjacent images. Many people will panic as they begin to wonder what most deserves attention at a time when the Great Calendar no longer excludes anything but calls instead for everything to be reexamined. Then, if not before, people will realize how effectively the Great Calendar has channeled agendas during the final decades of the twentieth century.

Assuming that postmodern delight in juxtaposing opposites lasts until the year 2000, new techniques of selection will have to emerge. By then, people must learn to decide for themselves what merits commemoration, because public consensus will have collapsed under the sheer weight of available topics. In a foreboding of such overload, the bicentennial of the French Revolution elicited personal choice as many citizens criticized managers' decisions about which events to commemorate. At ceremonies performed by thousands of actors, officials chose to reenact at Versailles on May 4, 1989, the assembling of the Estates General (which was telescoped with the Oath of the Tennis Court, an event that took place nearly seven weeks later). The exclusivity of the guest list at that evening's gala offended many. In Paris both on July 14 and again on August 26 actors recreated the proclamation of the Declaration of the Rights of Man and the Citizen. Although the latter ceremony was aimed at attracting youth around the world, Britain's Mrs. Thatcher was not the only authority questioning to what extent France, rather than the United States (or less plausibly Great Britain), had pioneered the notion of civil rights for all. Even though the Storming of the Bastille was not reenacted, it was recalled through the inauguration on July 13 of a new Opera House at the Place de la Bastille. The inappropriateness of inviting world leaders to celebrate a popular uprising by attending the opera preoccupied the Paris press for weeks.

Notwithstanding these extravanganzas, the public manifested disillusionment from the start of the bicentennial. Not just in areas ravaged by the Jacobins but elsewhere as well, many preferred to recall the valor of counterrevolutionaries or the allure of customs that the Revolution assailed. Many communities refused to plant trees of liberty as they were bidden to do on March 21. Plans to recreate the atmosphere of the gardens of the Palais Royal, which throughout 1789 had witnessed popular gatherings, foundered for lack of interest. Towns in the West collaborated to finance a film dramatizing the horrors of Jacobin suppression, and at the Chateau of Puy du Fou fourteen communes staged a drama deploring the Jacobins' wars in the Vendée. On August 15, 1989, a day once celebrated as Napoleon's birthday, Catholics attended mass for victims of the Revolution. If the bicentennial did not command the degree of consensus that planners had hoped for, this is partly because Europeans now interpret history in more individualistic ways. Fewer citizens want cultural managers telling them what to commemorate. The bicentennial opened divisions more than it healed them, as personal and regional pantheons begin to replace public ones.

If the bicentennial of the French Revolution could not command consensus, one trembles to think how the bimillennium will fan diversity. In a year when all anniversaries coincide, no single one will impose conformity. One recoils in bewilderment before the prospect of trying to program the bimillennium in the manner of the Revolutionary bicentennial. The task of selecting high points, or even low points, for attention, whether in world capitals or villages, will defeat the ablest of planners. In the year 2000 there can be no hope of eliciting a consensus in even one city, much less one country, as to what most deserves attention. Any attempt to impose consensus will unloose a backlash. If nothing else does, the oversupply of celebrands will awaken bimillennial consciousness.

How can managers who have been commemorating one year's quota at a time suddenly cope with several thousand years' worth? The riches of the Great Calendar will get telescoped into something like Jorge Luis Borges's conceit of the Library of Babel, in which all the world becomes a library.[5] Equally daunting, in the year 2000 all history will undergo commemoration. The bimillennium promises to turn into a hypercommemoration, a grand finale to two or three decades of postmodern anniversary fever. Everything that has been commemorated since the 1960s, and all else besides, will come up for reappraisal in one grand burst of commemorativeness. The satisfaction that *homo rhythmicus* derives from experiencing recurrence at regular intervals will vanish for a year, and lack of repeatability will only heighten the tension.

If we think of the bimillennium as distilling all previous commemorations, a working principle for coping with it emerges: consumers will have to choose for themselves. The task can be likened to the challenge a composer faces when devising an overture for an opera. Which tunes deserve a place in the prelude? Which celebrands whose anniversaries came up during the previous fifty years (and by definition this includes everyone who ever lived) most deserve bimillennial attention? The difficulty of selecting bimillennial honorees shows that the Great Calendar will no longer suffice to impose consensus. Every planner, every intellectual, and indeed every citizen must propose his own bimillennial heroes, because the Great Calendar favors none in particular.

If the bimillennium accomplishes no other transformation, it will unmask the arbitariness of the Great Calendar as stabilizer of agendas. In the year 2000 every thinking person will have to ask himself or herself: Which figures and achievements from previous millennia most deserve commemorating? Just as the bimillennium will sharpen anxieties about ability to preserve the planet, so it will test capacity to remember the past. The anxious will ponder questions like: Which luminaries should be honored in the year 2100? And: How many people will feel inclined to commemorate anyone in the year 2500? The farsighted may even ask: Is there likely to be a trimillennium in the year 3000? Although managers routinely commemorate figures who lived five hundred or a thousand years ago, they may falter when contemplating similar spans in the future. If bimillennial celebrators are to juggle huge chunks of time with aplomb, they need to start practicing during the 1990s.

The impossibility of establishing consensus about whom to honor in the year 2000 pinpoints a cardinal trait of bimillennial consciousness. Where public agendas clash, everyone will be obliged to set priorities for himself. The Bimillennium will force people to seek new ways of affirming allegiances. Most likely, the cultural synthesizer that is the Great Calendar will evolve from enhancing public purposes to stimulating individuals, each in a different way. Each citizen will want to program his own synthesizer.

At present, cultural planners rely unthinkingly on the Great Calendar as a tool for generating consensus. Whether in defending or denouncing commemorations, intellectuals are obliged to react to what the Great Calendar imposes. Since the 1960s intellectuals have undertaken to reappraise the entire human past, working piecemeal as events and figures come up for anniversaries. The bimillennium will crown this process when everything comes up for reassessment in a single burst. The Age of Anniversaries will culminate in a grand finale that breaks all the rules, and the commemoration industry will stagger beneath a plethora of options.

Anniversaries during the Late 1990s

Some characteristics of the Giant Reappraisal can be discerned already. It will differ from previous commemorations, including massive ones such as the bicentennial of the French Revolution or the 500th of Columbus's first voyage, in the degree of awe it inspires. Whereas individual anniversaries sometimes sink into routine, the bimillennium will generate once-in-a-lifetime fervor, indeed once-in-a-thousand-years hyperactivity. The bimillennium stands apart in its power to induce awe in even the most jaded consumers. Anyone who casts his mind across even a small portion of the human saga since the year 1000 will feel alternately admiration and horror at the accomplishments and atrocities. Hardly anyone can react with indifference to such a panorama. Because postmoderns have tended to prefer in-souciance to awe, they need to start practicing it soon if the year 2000 is not to overwhelm them.[6]

Bimillennial awe, which quivers before the unimaginable scope of what awaits commemoration, needs to focus on a few individuals and events. No one can spend an entire year feeling intoxicated by the entirety of human achievement. Each person will have to single out a few individuals for special reverence or revulsion. A goal of com-memorations during the 1990s should be to encourage citizens to choose their own notables and detestables. If the privilege of selecting ancestors is to embolden instead of bewilder participants, they need to start choosing soon.

Of course not everyone will welcome the challenge of picking his or her own pantheon. Too many citizens have studied too little of the past to do so with confidence. As a safeguard, more needs to be done both in Europe and the United States to publicize events of previous turns-of-the-century so that people can ponder earlier upheavals, to-gether with their symbolism.[7] Someone should write *A Primer of Cultural History for the Bimillennium*, which would emphasize hap-penings during the 490s, the 990s, the 1490s, and the 1890s. Such a book would sketch historical cycles as a guide to envisioning changes of era. As the bimillennium nears, philosophy of history will win at-tention by helping people to think about a thousand years in one gulp.[8] Historical generalists may attract larger audiences than they do now, particularly if they tackle the sweep of global history.

Even though the cult of anniversaries may collapse under its own weight during the years 2000 and 2001, it can be used during the late 1990s to enhance bimillennial consciousness. It is not too early to start steering the celebrands of the late 1990s toward bimillennial themes. An ideal figure for evoking misgivings and hopes about the bimillennium is the French historian Jules Michelet (1798–1876), whose bicentennial in 1998 invites us to ponder historical vicissi-tudes. Michelet, who in 1855 introduced the concept of the Italian Renaissance that Jacob Burckhardt publicized five years later, spe-cialized in charting ups and downs in a way that everyone can under-stand.[9] His gift for dramatizing history and his alertness to opportuni-ties that got missed make him a model popularizer. He understood how people respond to symbols, including the symbolism of the cal-endar. Conferences held in 1998 on how Michelet might have interpreted both the year 1900 and the year 2000 could stimulate discussion on all the questions raised in this book. Because history as a pillar of national identity and as a spur to reform was his stock-in-trade, Michelet will preside splendidly over the waning of the twentieth century.

A bleaker anniversary in 1998 is that of Thomas Malthus's prophetic book *An Essay on the Principle of Population* (1798). The Anglican curate's vision of population outstripping food supply has haunted theories of development ever since. Not for nothing did Malthus help earn for economics the nickname of the "dismal science." His influence on Marx, Darwin, and advocates of birth control makes his a pivotal text for reappraising threats to the environment. Already mankind faces a Malthusian crisis, as more and more billions of people demand resources. To assess Malthus's gloom in conjunction with Michelet's cheer will make a heady confrontation. Michelet and Malthus personify what will probably be two principal responses to the bimillennium: soaring optimism and relentless pessimism. To juxtapose these alternatives at a co-commemoration in 1998 would pinpoint issues for the year 2000.

During 1999 an astonishing roster of geniuses will come up for commemoration. The cult of anniversaries bids fair to close the century in a burst of glory. Among supreme masters to be commemorated are three great painters: the Spaniard Diego Velázquez (1599–1660), the Fleming Anthony Van Dyck (1599–1641), and the Frenchman Jean-Baptiste-Siméon Chardin (1699–1779). The first two achieved perfection of style in a way that heralds the end of a century. Velázquez had no successors, and Van Dyck carried the court portrait to an apogee at the court of Charles I on the eve of its dissolution in the 1640s. Chardin, by way of contrast, shunned court circles, affirming an independence that suits bimillennial commitment to thinking for oneself.

An Italian painter of lesser gifts, Alessandro Magnasco (1667–1749), suits the eve of the bimillennium through his very elusiveness. His images of enigmatic monks and lightning-dazzled landscapes make him one of the most puzzling figures in Italian art. Vacillation between bitterness and humor, preference for baffling images, and refusal to adopt conventional roles attune him to the anxiety of a turn-of-the-millennium. People suffering a sense of bewilderment could not ask for a more suitable figure to embody it. An exhibition of

Magnasco's oeuvre will mark a fitting farewell to the twentieth century.

Among writers, four giants come up for reappraisal. The German demi-god Goethe (1749–1832) encompassed the learned culture of his period in a way that ever since has defied emulation. Goethe's comprehensiveness and capacity to grow make him a model for facing the bimillennium with serenity. Moreover, no one has occasioned more intense anniversary commemorations than did Goethe in Germany between 1882 and 1949. This makes him an ideal figure to round off the twentieth century. Since his anniversaries were commemorated with panache in 1882, 1899, 1932, 1949, and to a lesser extent in 1982, a survey of attitudes expressed on those occasions would offer a worthy epitaph to the Age of Anniversaries.

The French will have two giants to commemorate. Their quintessential dramatist Jean Racine (1639–1699) comes up again after having been somewhat overshadowed during the bicentennial of the French Revolution. As usual, he will occasion reflections about the past and future of French identity as expressed through literature. Racine will also justify viewing the bimillennium as a conflict between passion and duty. He will prod people to ask: Should one commemorate the bimillennium even if one feels no passion for it? Debates in his dramas about yielding to conformity may help some to resist it.

One of the greatest of French novelists, Honoré de Balzac (1799–1850), suits the bimillennium in several ways. Balzac discerned how the passion of the French Revolution for justice and fame had degenerated by the 1830s into lust for wealth and prestige. His historical novel, *Le Dernier chouan* (1829), one of the first of its kind in French, evoked the petering out of the Revolution among zealots unwilling to accept the end of the saga that had ennobled and besmirched so many lives. Similar inertia will no doubt haunt the end of the century. Moreover, Balzac's analysis of social classes can deepen understanding of the changes that the twentieth century has brought. If Racine etched conflicts between inclination and obligation, Balzac embedded these in a wealth of historical detail. Racine expounded principles, where Balzac narrated consequences for capitalist society. Between them, they forged tools for interpreting the awe-inspiring perspectives that the year 2000 will unfurl. Finally, what bimillennial consumers will need above all is mental energy; like Goethe, Balzac exuded an energy that took all experience for its province.

England's chief writer to be commemorated is the poet Edmund Spenser (c. 1552–1599). Apart from his mastery of versification, his role in 1999 will be to model the role of commemorator. His poem *The Faerie Queen* (1590–1596) offered a paean of praise to the England of Queen Elizabeth I, exalting her person and the panache of her courtiers. Through mellifluous language, delicate flattery, and unabashed declaration of awe, Spenser shows how to express admiration for whatever is truly admirable. By the year 1999 people will need to practice the arts of admiration as a step in selecting personal pantheons. To contemplate a great poet exuding admiration for his contemporaries will buoy intellectuals as they tremble at the end of one millennium gazing into the next.

In 1999 Italy will commemorate the 500th anniversary of the Platonic philosopher Marsilio Ficino (1433–1499). Although his combination of Christianity and Platonism may suit the ecumenicism of the bimillennium, Ficino's philosophizing will probably get overwhelmed by political anniversaries. England will be commemorating the demise of no less than three ill-fated kings. Richard I the Lion-Hearted died in 1199 at a siege in France; Richard II died in prison in 1399; and Charles I died on the scaffold in 1649. The memory of these vicissitudes will suffice to glamorize royalty, not least because monarchy will assure a sense of stability on the brink of the third millennium. The execution of Charles I will gain drama from the fact that his adversary Oliver Cromwell (1599–1658) will enjoy a 400th anniversary that same year. Joint conferences on Charles I and Cromwell may well resemble those of 1989 on William and Mary and the Glorious Revolution of 1688–1689. The theme of Burkean continuity will predominate.

In France the major political anniversary will be that of Napoleon I's seizure of power in 1799. Napoleon's accomplishments, of course, will need no rehearsal, but in a year when people will want to affirm continuity, the French will probably emphasize his role in perfecting the bureaucratized state that has thrived ever since. The French and indeed the European systems of law, administration, and education all bear the stamp of Napoleon. To acclaim the stability that his creations furnished to a nation whose political regimes changed more than a dozen times after that will appease many in 1999. By then, most likely, France will be so fully integrated into Europe that Napoleon will be hailed as a visionary of European unification as well. Equally significant in this regard will be the centennial of the first International Peace Conference that convened in The Hague in 1899. One may hope that by 1999 the 100th anniversary of an initiative to prevent wars will not seem as futile as its 50th did in 1949.

Conclusion: An Exhortation to Anticipate the Year 2000

As these examples show, political anniversaries seldom stimulate the same degree of innovation as do those of cultural figures like Goethe or Michelet. Cultural anniversaries will probably draw an ever-greater share of attention as the bimillennium approaches, for past politics has relatively little to say about a transition that affects all mankind. Europeans, with their predilection for cultural anniversaries, may adapt more readily to bimillennial exigencies than do Americans, who have preferred political anniversaries as an epitome of their civil religion. Above all, the bimillennium will force citizens to realize that they must choose for themselves which figures to venerate. Citizens can no longer leave the task of selection to courtier-managers, for too much is at stake in transmitting the human legacy beyond the year 2000.

This book began by emphasizing the role of anniversaries in cementing national and regional identity throughout Europe and the United States. The mundane function of reminding educated Europeans about culture-carriers who get read in secondary school underpins the cult of anniversaries as it is presently practiced. This book has argued that buttressing national identity will give way during the 1990s to preparing citizens to cope with the bimillennium. Increasingly, people will want to reinterpret national heritage in the light of entire centuries, and even millennia. Because this task surpasses the scope of even teams of managers, it will fall by default to each individual as a personal vocation.

The cult of anniversaries has thrived as a tool of cultural administrators during an era of transition. As other institutions for transmitting culture (such as schools, churches, and clubs) have lost authority, the cult of anniversaries has emerged to fill a vacuum left by the waning of consensus in cultural life. At present, anniversary commemorations undertake to proclaim attitudes toward the past and to assess what features of it deserve to be perpetuated. Increasingly, however, the question of commemorative priorities will pose itself for individuals and not just for administrators. The Great Calendar that throws up a roster of celebrands each year will evolve from a device for setting public agendas into a tool for helping each individual to choose personal favorites.

Both idealism and anxiety will proliferate at the end of the 1990s. The task of anniversary planners in the next decade will be to channel that uneasiness into productive paths. As the press, electronic media, and travel industry combine to focus attention worldwide on issues of change and continuity, intellectuals need to confront broader issues. The cult of anniversaries has brought the most diverse thinkers and artists under scrutiny. The challenge of the 1990s will be to focus the same range of thinkers on issues of survival and renewal in the twenty-first century. If co-commemorations, with their arbiters of commemorations, can help people to interpret creators in fresh ways, then everyone can embark toward the bimillennium with new horizons in view. If, however, cultural managers continue to exploit anniversaries as a mere expedient that lacks any vision of where mankind is heading, then commemorations will forfeit the consensus they command. If anniversaries prove disappointing, *homo rhythmicus* can seek other gratifications once the Great Divide of the year 2000 has passed.

The Age of Anniversaries has trifled long enough with a sense of aimlessness. It is time to harness its creativity to address questions about the future. The cult of anniversaries needs to move beyond resuscitating figures for a year and begin to invent ways of making each year's celebrands answer new questions and confront new challenges. The commemoration industry needs to generate bimillennial initiatives. If cultural managers do not prepare adequately for the bimillennium, the Great Calendar will take matters out of their hands when the year 2000 exposes the arbitrariness of today's conventions. It is too soon, however, to despair. Because the Age of Anniversaries has accustomed everyone to heed the Great Calendar, there is reason to hope that efforts to anticipate the new century will captivate planners and citizens alike. Already discourse about the twenty-first century is blossoming, and soon it will spawn a major industry.

The postmodern era has brought flexibility and ingenuity to reappraising the past. The next challenge will be to bring similar open-mindedness to confronting the bimillennium. If people show that they can rethink the French Revolution and Columbus's first voyage in startling ways, surely they can devote similar resourcefulness to contemplating the next century. All the anniversaries of the past twenty-five years have been preparing people for the Great Reappraisal that lies ahead. The anniversaries that will matter in 1998, 1999, and 2000 will grow out of those of the early 1990s. Now is the time to plan how to make these occasions matter. It is not too soon to begin practicing bimillennial consciousness. Those who neglect it will be alarmed instead of buoyed by the upsurge of hopefulness and anxiety that will sweep the globe during the next ten years. Before too long, the Age of Anniversaries itself may need to be commemorated.

Notes

1. David Lowenthal, *The Past Is a Foreign Country* (New York: Cambridge University Press, 1985), which takes at least half of its hundreds of examples from the British Isles. Patrick Wright, *On Living in an Old Century: The National Past in Contemporary Britain* (London, Verso, 1985) presents a more caustic view.
2. Stephen Toulmin, *Cosmopolis: The Hidden Agenda of Modernity* (New York: Free Press, 1990), pp. 1–4, 203–205.
3. A book that celebrates this propensity is Guy Scarpetta, *L'Impureté* (Paris: Grasset, 1985). He sees postmodern delight in unforeseen combinations as a revival of baroque, and more particularly of rococo, propensities.
4. Michel-Eugène Chevreul, *De la loi du contraste simultané des couleurs* (Paris, 1839), translated as *The Principles of Harmony and Contrast of Colors and Their Application to the Arts* (New York: Reinhold, 1967).
5. Jorge Luis Borges, "The Library of Babel" in *Labyrinths: Selected Stories and Other Writings* (New York: New Directions, 1964), pp. 51–58.
6. An eloquent debunker of awe is Jean Baudrillard, whose equation of postmodernism with deflation of all enthusaiams can be expected to fade as the year 2000 approaches. See Jean Baudrillard, *Selected Writings*, Mark Poster, ed. (Stanford: Stanford University Press, 1988).
7. See Hillel Schwartz, "Millenarianism: An Overview," *Encyclopedia of Religion*, 9 (1987): 521–532, on movements that envision an end of one world as foreshadowing the advent of another.
8. A bold philosophic history is Ernest Gellner, *Plough, Sword and Book: The Structure of Human History* (London: Collins Harvill, 1988).
9. Jules Michelet, *La Renaissance* in *Histoire de France*, vol. 7 (Paris, 1855) was followed by Jacob Burckhardt, *Die Cultur der Renaissance in Italien* (1860). On Michelet's versatility, see Linda Orr, *Jules Michelet: Nature, History, and Language* (Ithaca: Cornell University Press, 1976); Arthur Mitzman, *Michelet, Historian: Rebirth and Romanticism in Nineteenth-Century France* (New Haven: Yale University Press, 1990).

Bibliography

Key Concepts: National Identity, Civil Religion, Calendars

Boerner, Peter, ed., *Concepts of National Identity: An Interdisciplinary Dialogue* (Baden-Baden: Nomos, 1986) [conceptual essays on national identity in Europe].

Hobsbawm, Eric, and Terence Ranger, eds., *The Invention of Tradition* (Cambridge: Cambridge University Press, 1983) [essays analyzing the deliberate fashioning of traditions to buttress national identity during the nineteenth century].

James, Harold, *A German Identity, 1770–1990* (New York: Routledge, 1989) [analyses modes of national identity].

Lowenthal, David, *The Past Is a Foreign Country* (Cambridge: Cambridge University Press, 1985) [charts diverse modes of encountering the past, particularly in Britain].

Richey, Russell E., and Donald G. Jones, eds., *American Civil Religion* (New York: Harper and Row, 1974) [seminal essays on the concept of civil religion].

Wilcox, Donald J., *The Measure of Times Past: Pre-Newtonian Chronologies and the Rhetoric of Relative Time* (Chicago: University of Chicago Press, 1987) [documents alternative systems of dating from antiquity to Newton].

Zerubavel, Eviatar, *Hidden Rhythms: Schedules and Calendars in Social Life* (Chicago: University of Chicago Press, 1981) [expounds the need for calendric rhythms as a given of human behavior].

— — — — —, *The Seven Day Circle: The History and Meaning of the Week* (New York: Free Press, 1985) [exploits the phenomenon of the week to illustrate human craving for cycles].

Postmodernism

Connor, Steven, *Postmodernist Culture: An Introduction to Theories of the Contemporary* (Oxford: Basil Blackwell, 1989) [discerning analysis of competing theories, with a superb bibliography].

Hassan, Ihab, *The Postmodern Turn: Essays in Postmodern Theory and Culture* (Columbus: Ohio State University Press, 1987) [collection of essays by a literary critic who pioneered the notion of postmodernism in the early 1970s].

Lyotard, Jean-François, *The Postmodern Condition: A Report on Knowledge* [1979] (Minneapolis: University of Minnesota Press, 1984) [deplores the cognitive disarray that results from breakdown of authoritative conceptual structures].

Scarpetta, Guy, *L'Impureté* (Paris: Grasset, 1985) [salutes postmodernism as a neo-baroque blending of incongruous components].

Toulmin, Stephen, *Cosmopolis: The Hidden Agenda of Modernity* (New York: Free Press, 1990) [interprets postmodernism as ushering in the "Third Phase of Modernity"].

History of Commemorations

Nora, Pierre, ed., *Les Lieux de mémoire,* vol I. *La République* (Paris: Gallimard, 1984), pp. 381–591.

Ozouf, Mona, *Festivals and the French Revolution* (Cambridge: Harvard University Press, 1988).

Rydell, Robert W., *All the World's A Fair: Visions of Empire at American International Expositions, 1876–1916* (Chicago: University of Chicago Press, 1984).

Sanson, Rosamonde, *Les 14 juillet (1789–1975): Fête et consciences nationales* (Paris: Flammarion, 1976).

Schulz, Uwe, ed., *Das Fest von der Antike bis zur Gegenwart* (Munich: Beck, 1989).

Compilations of Dates

Delorme, Jean, *Chronologie des civilisations,* 2d ed. (Paris: Presses Universitaires de France, 1969) [parallel charts of dates in world history].

Gregory, Ruth W., *Anniversaries and Holidays* (Chicago: American Library Association, 1983) [month-by-month calendar of fixed days and movable days in the United States, with ample bibliography].

Grun, Bernard, *The Timetables of History: A Horizontal Linkage of People and Events,* 2d ed. (New York: Simon and Schuster, 1982) [elegant parallel charts of world history].

Hatch, Jane M., ed., *The American Book of Days,* 3d ed. (New York: Wilson, 1978) [day-by-day classification of thousands of American anniversaries and celebrations].

Haydn, Joseph T., *Haydn's Dictionary of Dates and Universal Information Relating to All Ages and Nations*, revised by Benjamin Vincent, 25th ed. (New York: Putnam, 1911) [exotic information about first occurrences, up to 1910, arranged alphabetically by place, concept, and persons].

Langer, William L., ed., *An Encyclopedia of World History, Ancient, Medieval, and Modern*, 5th ed. (Boston: Houghton Mifflin, 1973) [the classic compilation of world history arranged by country and year].

Thorne, J.O., ed., *Chambers's Biographical Dictionary*, rev. ed. (New York: St. Martin's Fress, 1974) [over 15,000 brief biographies from all cultures].

Williams, Neville, *Chronology of the Modern World: 1763 to the Present Time* (London: Barrie and Rockliff, 1966) [chronicles the period 1763–1963 year by year, with details on art, literature, and science in all countries].

Index